S. Hrg. 113–646

HEARING ON THE REPORT OF THE PRESIDENT'S REVIEW GROUP ON INTELLIGENCE AND COMMUNICATIONS TECHNOLOGIES

HEARING

BEFORE THE

COMMITTEE ON THE JUDICIARY UNITED STATES SENATE

ONE HUNDRED THIRTEENTH CONGRESS

SECOND SESSION

TUESDAY, JANUARY 14, 2014

Serial No. J–113–46

Printed for the use of the Committee on the Judiciary

U.S. GOVERNMENT PUBLISHING OFFICE

94–477 PDF   WASHINGTON : 2015

For sale by the Superintendent of Documents, U.S. Government Publishing Office
Internet: bookstore.gpo.gov   Phone: toll free (866) 512–1800; DC area (202) 512–1800
Fax: (202) 512–2104   Mail: Stop IDCC, Washington, DC 20402–0001

COMMITTEE ON THE JUDICIARY

PATRICK J. LEAHY, Vermont, *Chairman*

DIANNE FEINSTEIN, California
CHUCK SCHUMER, New York
DICK DURBIN, Illinois
SHELDON WHITEHOUSE, Rhode Island
AMY KLOBUCHAR, Minnesota
AL FRANKEN, Minnesota
CHRISTOPHER A. COONS, Delaware
RICHARD BLUMENTHAL, Connecticut
MAZIE HIRONO, Hawaii

CHUCK GRASSLEY, Iowa, *Ranking Member*
ORRIN G. HATCH, Utah
JEFF SESSIONS, Alabama
LINDSEY GRAHAM, South Carolina
JOHN CORNYN, Texas
MICHAEL S. LEE, Utah
TED CRUZ, Texas
JEFF FLAKE, Arizona

KRISTINE LUCIUS, *Chief Counsel and Staff Director*
KOLAN DAVIS, *Republican Chief Staff Director*

CONTENTS

STATEMENTS OF COMMITTEE MEMBERS

WITNESSES

QUESTIONS

ANSWERS

SUBMISSIONS FOR THE RECORD

ADDITIONAL SUBMISSIONS FOR THE RECORD

IV

HEARING ON THE REPORT OF THE PRESIDENT'S REVIEW GROUP ON INTELLIGENCE AND COMMUNICATIONS TECHNOLOGIES

TUESDAY, JANUARY 14, 2014

U.S. SENATE,
COMMITTEE ON THE JUDICIARY,
Washington, DC.

The Committee met, pursuant to notice, at 2:30 p.m., in Room SD–226, Dirksen Senate Office Building, Hon. Patrick J. Leahy, Chairman of the Committee, presiding.

Present: Senators Leahy, Feinstein, Durbin, Whitehouse, Klobuchar, Franken, Coons, Blumenthal, Grassley, Sessions, Graham, Lee, and Cruz.

OPENING STATEMENT OF HON. PATRICK J. LEAHY, A U.S. SENATOR FROM THE STATE OF VERMONT

Chairman LEAHY. We have a roll call vote expected soon, but I wanted to get this started, and then when the vote occurs at some point, we can recess for a few minutes while we go and vote.

But what is important about this hearing, we are going to hear from the President's Review Group on Intelligence and Communications Technologies. I was talking briefly with them in the back, and I know this is the first time they have appeared together publicly since their ground-breaking report was released last month, and I thank them, as I know the President has and others have, for taking the time, a lot of time, and effort to prepare this report. And I know it will be reflective of what the President is going to say later this week.

The Review Group's report addresses some of the weightiest issues that are going to confront us in the coming years. We know what the technology is today. None of us can predict what it is going to be five to 10 years from now. And we also know that more and more data will be created by all of us as each day passes. And the questions are obvious: When should our government be allowed to collect and use that data? To what extent does the massive collection of data improve our national security? And what will the answers to these questions mean for privacy and free expression in the 21st century?

All three branches of government are grappling with whether to let the NSA's dragnet collection of Americans' domestic phone records continue, and we are finally doing so with full public participation in that debate.

I think Americans across the political spectrum want us to have this debate and want to have a clearer understanding of what is going on, so we are trying to get as much as we can into a public hearing. All of us on this Committee have had access, as have the five witnesses, to highly classified matters, but we are trying to go into as much as we can in open session.

The most critical factor in deciding whether to conduct any particular intelligence activity is an assessment of its value. This is particularly important in evaluating the phone records program conducted under Section 215 of the *USA PATRIOT Act*. As I have said repeatedly, I have concluded that this phone records program is not uniquely valuable enough to justify the massive intrusion on Americans' privacy.

The Review Group likewise concluded that the program has not been essential, saying, and I will quote the Review Group: "The information contributed to terrorist investigations by the use of section 215 telephony metadata was not essential to preventing attacks and could readily have been obtained in a timely manner using conventional section 215 orders." And a few pages later, they said: "Section 215 has generated relevant information in only a small number of cases, and there has been no instance in which NSA could say with confidence that the outcome would have been different without the section 215 telephony metadata program."

The report explains that nothing in Section 215, as interpreted by the FISA Court, would preclude the mass collection of Americans' personal information beyond phone records.

The privacy implications of this sort of massive surveillance in the digital age cannot be overstated, and the Review Group's report provides some very valuable insights. The report appropriately questions whether we can continue to draw a rational line between metadata and content, and I think that is a critically important question given that many of our surveillance laws depend upon the distinction between the two.

These insights are also important as we take up reforms to the National Security Letter (NSL) statutes. We do not talk as much about the National Security Letters, but using them, the FBI can obtain detailed information about individuals' communications records, financial transactions, and credit reports without judicial approval. But the thing that is troubling to many is that recipients of NSLs are subject to permanent gag orders. Senator Durbin and I have been fighting to impose additional safeguards on this controversial authority for years—to limit their use, to ensure that NSL gag orders comply with the First Amendment, and to provide recipients of NSLs with a meaningful opportunity for judicial review—something that most Americans would assume already exists. And the Review Group report makes a series of important recommendations to change the way National Security Letters operate. We have not seen as much about these recommendations in the press. They have not generated as much attention, but they should. And I think that we have to look at them.

The report also recommends creating an institutional Public Interest Advocate at the FISA Court. I strongly support that proposal. I am concerned that merely allowing for an amicus to participate at the FISA Court from time to time will neither improve the substantive outcome of the proceedings, nor rebuild public confidence in the process. And the stakes are high.

When you think about it, we are really having a debate about what are Americans' fundamental relationship with their own government. The government exists for Americans, not the other way around, and we must debate whether the government should have the power to create massive data bases of information about its citizens. This is a feeling I would have no matter who is the head of our government.

I believe strongly that we must impose stronger limits on government surveillance powers, and I am confident that most Vermonters agree with me. I believe most Americans agree with me. Having said that, we want to do it right.

Now, on our panel today we will have Richard Clarke, who is the CEO of Good Harbor Security Risk Management. He is Chairman of the Board of Governors of the Middle East Institute. During his 30 years of public service, he was a senior White House National Security Adviser to Presidents George H.W. Bush, where I first met him, Bill Clinton, and George W. Bush.

Then we will have Michael Morell, who recently retired as the Deputy Director of the Central Intelligence Agency after more than 30 years of service, and during that time he served as Acting Director. He earned his bachelor's degree from the University of Akron and a master's degree from Georgetown.

And Geoffrey Stone currently serves as a professor at the University of Chicago Law School. He previously clerked for Supreme Court Justice William Brennan. And Professor Stone also served as dean of the University of Chicago Law School and a provost of the university.

Cass Sunstein is currently a professor at Harvard Law School, previously served as Administrator of the Office of Information and Regulatory Affairs. He also served as an attorney adviser at the Office of Legal Counsel, Department of Justice, and was a law clerk to Supreme Court Justice Thurgood Marshall.

And last, Professor Peter Swire is currently a professor at the Georgia Institute of Technology. He previously taught at Ohio State University's Moritz College of Law. In 2012, he was named to co-chair the Do Not Track standards process of the World Wide Web Consortium. He served as the Clinton administration's Chief Counsel for Privacy from 1999 to 2001.

Now, gentlemen, did you have a particular way you wished to proceed?

Mr. SUNSTEIN. After consultation with your staff, we have a very brief opening statement, if that is agreeable to you, Mr. Chairman.

Chairman Leahy. Go ahead.

STATEMENT OF THE HONORABLE CASS R. SUNSTEIN, THE HONORABLE RICHARD A. CLARKE, MICHAEL J. MORELL, GEOFFREY R. STONE, AND PETER SWIRE, THE PRESIDENT'S REVIEW GROUP ON INTELLIGENCE AND COMMUNICATIONS TECHNOLOGIES

Mr. SUNSTEIN. Well, notwithstanding our diversity, which you just signaled, we began this process with great admiration and gratitude for the intelligence community, and we would like to start by honoring their extraordinary work in keeping the Nation safe.

The risks associated with terrorism and associated threats are real, and one of our main goals has been to suggest reforms that are compatible with combating those risks.

After extensive discussions and consultations during the last months, the gratitude and admiration that we had for the intelligence community has only increased as a result of interacting with them. We found the highest levels of professionalism. We found no evidence of political or religious targeting or targeting people because of political dissent. Their focus has genuinely been on national security.

We are also grateful to them for their help and cooperation on a very tight time schedule, and they provided us with great access to information, making our report possible.

We are also grateful to many organizations and individuals—over two dozen, in fact—who actually met with us were concerned with technology and innovation, with privacy, with civil liberties, with freedom of the press, with the rights of journalists, with our relations with other nations, friendly nations and some that are not particularly friendly, but ensuring that our relations are as cooperative as possible. Countless organizations and individuals have devoted energy and time to informing our work, and we are grateful to them.

Much of our focus has been on maintaining the ability of the intelligence community to do what it needs to do, and we emphasize—if there is one thing to emphasize, it is this: that not one of the 46 recommendations in our report would, in our view, compromise or jeopardize that ability in any way.

On the contrary, many of the recommendations would strengthen that ability explicitly by increasing safeguards against insider threats and by eliminating certain gaps in the law that make it hard to track people under circumstances in which we have reason to believe they do not wish to do us well.

In terms of the reforms we favor, just three very general points.

The first is the immense importance of maintaining a free and open Internet, promoting both democratic and economic values. Across partisan lines there is a commitment to Internet freedom, and what is done in this domain, we believe, should be compatible with that commitment.

The second is the importance of risk management, signaled, I think, Mr. Chairman, by your opening remarks—that is a central unifying theme—considering multiple risks, first and foremost, the risk to national security, but including also the risk to public trust, risk to privacy, risk to economic values, and risk to democratic self-governance. So a major task going forward, what our report tries to thread a needle on, is try to ensure a full set of risks are taken into account and that we are not optimizing only along one dimension.

The third point is the importance of accountability, which is a unifying theme for our 46 recommendations—accountability to senior-level policy officials; accountability to the legal system, to Congress, and this Committee through increased transparency and disclosure; and above all to the American people through transparency and disclosure. And I should emphasize that one form of accountability includes steps that would help increase public trust not just within the United States but throughout the world.

This is a diverse group, as noted. We reached all of our recommendations—and this is a bit of an upset—by agreement. There are no dissents. There was no horse trading, and there was no compromising. There are 46——

Chairman LEAHY. You would never make it in the Senate.

[Laughter.]

Mr. SUNSTEIN. There are 46 recommendations. If my arithmetic is right, we have 230 votes. That is, all five of us are behind all 46 recommendations.

No team bats a thousand or even comes close, and our transmittal letter makes clear to the intelligence community, to this Committee, to the American people that we offer our recommendations with a great deal of humility and as a mere part of a process, prominently including the deliberations and judgments of this Committee.

We look forward to your questions.

[The prepared statement of the President's Review Group appears as a submission for the record.]

Chairman LEAHY. Well, thank you very much, and I noticed that in the comment I made, I think a couple things are extraordinary here: one, that you did reach such consensus, and I wish we could reach the same kind of consensus in the Senate—on many things we do, but not enough. And, second, your comments about the professionalism of our intelligence community, the men and women in our various intelligence communities, I totally agree with you. As Mr. Morell knows, without going into the subject of some of our closed-door briefings, he has heard both Republicans and Democrats praise the work on some of the things he has had to bring before us, some very critical matters. And I have spent enough time with station chiefs around the world in different places and realize how important the work that they all do is.

Now, when the bulk phone records program was made public last year, there were some who immediately began arguing that the program was critical to national security. They cited 54 terrorist plots being thwarted. Now, you have had reason to review those 54 examples, as I have. As I read the report, it reaches the same conclusion that I and others here did: that the Section 215 program contributed to only a few of those cases and was not essential to preventing any terrorist attacks.

I think it is also important to look at another thing we keep hearing—that somehow if this program had been in place before 9/11, it could have prevented that.

Now, Mr. Clarke, you were a senior counterterrorism official at the time of those attacks. Would the bulk phone records program have prevented 9/11?

Mr. CLARKE. Senator, I think it is impossible to go back and reconstruct history. I think while "what if" history is interesting academically, it is very difficult to say with accuracy if one fact had been changed, that the outcome would have been significantly different.

I think we can say this: that if the information that the federal agencies had at the time had been shared among the agencies, then one of them, the FBI, could have gone to the FISA Court and could have, in a very timely manner, gotten a warrant to monitor the appropriate telephones. They did not because they were unaware of the information that existed elsewhere in the government at the time. But there was a period of over two years where that information was available, so it would have been possible, in a very timely manner, to get a warrant from the FISA Court.

Chairman LEAHY. Wasn't that one of the things that Senator Graham and his review committee found, that was the sharing?

Mr. CLARKE. That is exactly right. The Joint Committee, the two Intelligence Committees of the House and Senate, found that the information was in the government at the time; it just was not shared.

Chairman LEAHY. Now, I raised the issue of National Security Letters, or NSLs, and as you know, and for those who are not familiar, they permit the government to obtain certain communications and financial and credit report records without a court order. Also, as I raised, the FBI can impose a virtually permanent gag order on NSL recipients. A number of us have been trying to reform that. Your recommendations on NSLs have not had as much attention as other topics covered by the report, but I think they are just as important.

So, Professor Swire, how did the Review Group arrive at its conclusions regarding NSLs?

Mr. SWIRE. Thank you, Mr. Chairman. Well, we arrived at it— the group amongst us includes three law professors, so on legal matters we were particularly involved. We went to the FBI, and we interviewed FBI counsel in detail. We also amongst us had worked quite a bit on issues related to NSLs previously.

Based on that, one of the things we focused on was the so-called gag orders or nondisclosure orders. In the criminal world, when there is an organized crime investigation, there are often nondisclosure orders on the order of 45 or 60 days. We found out that they are either permanent or come up for review for the first time in 50 years under current law for NSLs, and that is very, very different from the way that grand jury subpoenas or investigations on the criminal side happen. And so that lack of disclosure and the long, long period of secrecy is certainly one thing we were concerned about.

Chairman LEAHY. Well, doesn't that create a real problem in some cases for the person receiving the NSL, the gag order?

Mr. SWIRE. Well, so it poses problems for the email providers, phone companies who receive the NSLs, where they are not in a position to describe what activities they are taking. That can lead to situations where, among other things, the actual facts might be quite reasonable if understood more broadly. Many of the providers have expressed concern that they, under this gag order, cannot reassure their customers about the good practices that exist, and that has been a concern for the industry, certainly.

Chairman LEAHY. Well, before I yield to Senator Grassley, Professor Sunstein, let me ask you. Some would say the NSLs are like a grand jury subpoena, and you can have the gag order, there is not judicial review and so on. Do you agree with that?

Mr. SUNSTEIN. There is an overlap, and the FBI has been driving that analogy. There is also another analogy, which is Section 215 itself, where we recommend a certain process that is more consistent with the normal one for getting access to people's records. We think that if 215 has the structure that it should, then the National Security Letter should follow the same structure, that the separation between them is extremely hard to justify.

There is a certain analogy to the administrative subpoena. There is a question of breadth and scope with respect to National Security Letters, and we think that given the emergency exception that, of course, there would be, that to treat the National Security Letter like a 215 record seeking would not compromise any national security goal.

Chairman LEAHY. Thank you, and I thank Senator Grassley for letting me ask just one more question.

I will say this to Mr. Morell. We have heard some government officials talk about the Section 215 program; they say we should not—Americans should not—be concerned about it because the phone records the NSA obtains are just metadata and not particularly sensitive. The Review Group said there were some risks posed by the government obtaining massive amounts of metadata. Could you just elaborate on that a little bit?

Mr. MORELL. Well, I will say one of the things that I learned in this process, that I came to realize in this process, Mr. Chairman, is that there is quite a bit of content in metadata. When you have the records of the phone calls that a particular individual made, you can learn an awful lot about that person, and that is one of the things that struck me. So there is not, in my mind, a sharp distinction between metadata and content. It is more of a continuum.

Chairman LEAHY. In fact, in the *New York Times* op-ed, the five of you wrote, "The government should end its domestic program for storing bulk telephone metadata. The current program creates potential risks to public trust, personal privacy, and civil liberty." And, of course, the concern I have had and some others have had, no matter who is President or who is the head of these agencies, we do not want the temptation in there to misuse it.

Senator Grassley, thank you for coming over, and I would note that Senators have been joining us. I think we were all told there was going to be a vote at 2:30, and apparently that has not happened. If we keep looking over your head, we are looking at those little white dots up on the clock to see when the next one might be.

Senator Grassley, go ahead.

OPENING STATEMENT OF HON. CHUCK GRASSLEY, A U.S. SENATOR FROM THE STATE OF IOWA

Senator GRASSLEY. The Chairman just explained what I wanted to explain, that you folks may not think this is a very important hearing, but it is a very important hearing, but you may not conclude that since other Members are not here. But we were all told that there was going to be a vote at 2:30.

Before I ask questions, I have an opportunity to give an opening statement. I thank all of you for being here and for your work on the Committee.

This is the latest in a series of hearings on government surveillance authorities that our Committee has held. The NSA continues to be of great concern to my constituents and many across our country.

The most important responsibility of government is to protect our national security, while at the same time preserving our civil liberties. This is a responsibility that is quite hard to meet. Rapid changes in technology are making our enemies more lethal, our world more interconnected, and our privacy more subject to possible intrusion.

Under these circumstances, it is useful to hear a variety of perspectives, including from those outside government, and I thank the members of the Review Group for your service.

Some of the conclusions in the Review Group's report may help clarify the issues before us as we consider possible reforms.

First, according to the report, ''Although recent disclosures and commentary have created the impression in some quarters that NSA surveillance is indiscriminate and pervasive across the globe, that is not the case.'' Then the report concludes, I quote again, ''We have not uncovered any official efforts to suppress dissent or any intent to intrude into people's private lives without legal justification.''

None of this means that the potential for abuse of these authorities should not concern us—it should—or that the NSA has not made serious mistakes or that the law in this area could not be improved. Indeed, there is a place for additional transparency, safeguards, and oversight. But these conclusions are helpful in clarifying the issues.

Second, the report recommends that ''The national security of the United States depends on the continued capacity of NSA and other agencies to collect essential information. In considering proposals for reform, now and for the future, policymakers should avoid the risk of overreaction and take care in making changes that could undermine the capabilities of the Intelligence Community.'' And that is very good advice, folks.

One recommendation that may reflect this advice is the Review Group's proposal to preserve the government's controversial ability to query telephone metadata, but with some changes.

One of those recommended changes is that private entities hold the metadata. This is an interesting idea perhaps worth investigating. But I think it is legitimate to have concern that it may create as many privacy problems as it solves. Indeed, private companies seem to be allowing their customers' information to be hacked on what seems to be a daily basis.

Just as importantly, I am concerned that in other instances the Review Group may not have followed its own advice. Some of its other recommendations may seriously threaten our national security, if adopted collectively.

For example, some of the recommendations in the report appear to make it more difficult to investigate a terrorist than a common criminal. Some appear to extend the rights of Americans to foreigners without good reason. And some appear to rebuild the wall between our law enforcement and national security communities that existed before September 11, 2001. Of course, that wall helped contribute to our inability to detect and thwart the attacks on that day, and thousands died as a result.

I do not mean to criticize the effort or intentions of the Review Group. But I am concerned that the group was given such a relatively short time to do their work. As a result, for example, I understand the group spent only one day at the NSA. And if I am wrong on that, you can correct that.

I am also concerned that the group lacked some important perspectives. For example, none of the members has experience in supervising terrorism investigations at the Department of Justice or the FBI.

I am concerned that the group produced a large number of recommendations, but did not develop some of them fully.

As the Review Group wrote, its recommendations ''will require careful assessment by a wide range of relevant officials, with close reference to the likely consequences.'' That is pretty good advice, and I look forward to beginning that process today.

Now I have a question for Dr. Morell. After the Review Group issued its report, you wrote an opinion piece in which you emphasized that the report recommends changing the telephony metadata program rather than ending it. You wrote, ''Had the program been in place more than a decade ago, it would likely have prevented the September 11th terror attacks.'' Further, you wrote that the program ''has the potential to prevent the next 9/11.''

So my question: I would like to have you expand upon why you hold those two opinions. And also, can you give us any specific examples of how the metadata program was valuable to you when you headed the CIA?

Chairman LEAHY. Press the button.

Mr. MORELL. Senator, let me first say that the reason I wrote the op-ed, particularly with regard to 215, is I felt that there was a misperception on the part of the media and much of the American public that the Review Group had indeed recommended an end to the program. And we did not do that. We recommended a change in approach, and that was the main reason I wrote the op-ed, is to make that clear.

It is absolutely true that the 215 program has not played a significant role in disrupting any terrorist attacks to this point. That is a different statement than saying the program is not important. The program, as I said in the op-ed, only has to be successful once to be invaluable, and it does carry the potential going forward to prevent a catastrophic attack on the United States. And that was another point I was trying to make, and I believe it.

Another point I will make, Mr. Chairman, is that—and we talked about this as a group—there is value in a negative query of the 215 data. So if you have a terrorist overseas who is talking about an attack and you do not know where that attack is going to be, it is invaluable to query the 215 data base, and if the answer is that terrorist does not have any contacts in the United States, that gives you some reassurance that the attack will not be here. We talk about that in the report, and I think that is another important point.

Senator GRASSLEY. Thank you. For anyone, I have a question, but let me read a lead-in.

One of the changes that your report recommends concerning the telephony metadata program is that a private third party or parties hold the metadata instead of the NSA. But we have seen many recent instances where companies like Target and Neiman Marcus have been unable to protect private data. My constituents would be very concerned about privacy issues. So any one of you, but hopefully not all of you because I want to ask one more question, what was the group's assessment of the privacy risks associate with your recommendation that the metadata be stored in private hands? And did you speak to the telephone companies to explore whether they are willing or able to hold the metadata?

Mr. STONE. We did speak with the telephone companies about that, and they obviously would rather not hold that data. Our judgment about the government holding the data is that the primary danger of the 215 telephony metadata program is not if it is used only in the way in which its use is authorized, but that it leaves sitting out there a huge amount of information, personal information about Americans that could be abused in awful ways. And the question is how to avoid that potential abuse.

One of the ways we decided it makes sense to avoid that is to take it out of the hands of government. The concern of the Fourth Amendment, the concern of our constitutional history is that government can do far more harm if it abuses information in its possession than private entities can. And, therefore, our judgment was that the government should not have possession of this information because if it does, there is always the possibility of someone coming along down the road, seeing this as a great opportunity to get political dirt on individuals, on their activities, on their organizations, their associations, and that that is a danger that we want to avoid.

On the other hand, we do believe that the data is useful, and the idea was to find a way that would enable the government to have access to the data but minimize the risk that it could be abused in that way. And our judgment was that keeping it in private hands would still pose, as you say, privacy risks, but the privacy risks would be of a very different order, and they would be much less in the sense of the kind of abuse that historically we are most concerned about with the government.

Senator GRASSLEY. This will be my last question. One of the things that I am concerned about is that we not rebuild the wall that exists between our law enforcement and national security communities before September 11th. Part of that is making sure that we do not make it harder to investigate a terrorism case and any other type of crime. FBI Director Comey weighed in last week on reforms you proposed to national security. He called these letters ''a very important tool that is essential'' to the work of the FBI. He also stated, ''What worries me about the suggestion that we impose a judicial process on NSLs is that it would actually make it harder for us to do national security investigations than bank fraud investigations.''

Question to Professor Swire—maybe somebody else more appropriate, but whoever—why would we want to make it harder for agents and prosecutors to investigate espionage and terrorism than other crimes? Did you consult with Director Comey personally about these recommendations? And, finally, aren't your rec-

ommendations in this area almost exactly the same as what you—
I assume Professor Swire—recommended to this Committee back in
2007, long before the recent controversy about NSA?

Mr. SWIRE. Well, law professors are always thrilled if someone
reads their articles from several years ago, so it is true that I wrote
on FISA prior to that. It is also true that we went to the FBI, that
the FBI lawyers came to us, and that we met with Mr. Comey last
week to discuss these issues. So we have had quite extensive discussions.

In terms of the comparisons with criminal, any criminal investigation, of course, you have all the criminal powers, and then you
may also have the NSL and foreign intelligence authorities. There
are some differences. One difference is that in the criminal investigations, if there was some mistake or problem, that comes to
light, and there is a check and balance there. If you have 50 years
of secrecy, we never find out what the government is doing. And
so because of that risk of long-running secrecy and not knowing
what it is, some extra safeguards are appropriate for these secret
foreign intelligence things. That is at least one difference that exists.

Senator GRASSLEY. Okay.

Chairman LEAHY. Thank you. I am going to yield to the Chair
of the Senate Intelligence Committee, Senator Feinstein, but before
I do that, I just want to place in the record—and I meant to have
done this earlier—a detailed report published by the New America
Foundation that concludes the executive branch claims about the
effectiveness of Section 215 phone records are overblown, even mis-
leading; and then a new report by the Hoover Institution re-
searcher concluding that Section 215 phone records are only of
marginal value. Without objection, those will be placed in the
record.

[The information referred to appears as a submission for the
record.]

Chairman LEAHY. Again, I want to say how much we appreciate
that Senator Feinstein is a Member of this Committee with her expertise, and the other Members who also serve on the Intelligence
Committee in both parties. Senator Feinstein.

Senator FEINSTEIN. Well, thank you very much, Mr. Chairman.
I appreciate those comments.

I would like to submit a statement for the record, if I may.

Chairman LEAHY. Sure.

Senator GRASSLEY. Can I, at the same time, ask for something
to be put in the record?

Senator FEINSTEIN. Absolutely.

Chairman LEAHY. Without objection, the items by both Senator
Feinstein and Senator Grassley will be made part of the record.

[The prepared statement of Senator Feinstein appears as a submission for the record.]

[The information referred to appears as a submission for the
record.]

Senator FEINSTEIN. Thank you very much, Mr. Chairman.

Mr. Chairman, the Intelligence Committee—and I think virtually
every Member was there, perhaps missing one—had the opportunity of talking to the professorial element of this Committee last

week. The intelligence element was not there, and we very much regret that Mr. Clarke and Mr. Morell were not there. But, Mr. Morell, particularly for your ears, I think what we thought in reading the report and in listening to the testimony was that the group did not want the program to continue. And then I read your op-ed piece in the *Wall Street Journal*—excuse me, in the *Washington Post*, and I would just like to read parts of it and see if the Committee agrees, if I may.

"Several news outlets have reported that the review group had called for an end to the program, but we did not do that. We called for a change in approach rather than a wholesale rejection. To better protect the privacy and civil liberties of Americans—key values of our Republic—we recommended that the Government no longer hold the data and that it be required to obtain an individual court order"—which I want to ask you about—"for each search. But make no mistake: The review group reaffirmed that the program should remain a tool of our Government in the fight against terrorism."

Then you go on: "Another misperception involved the review group's view of the efficacy of Section 215; many commentators said it found no value in the program. The report accurately said that the program has not been 'essential'"—and I want to also talk about the word "essential"—"'to preventing attacks' since its creation. But that is not the same thing as saying the program is not important to national security, which is why we did not recommend its elimination."

Mr. Swire, do you agree with that, yes or no?

Mr. SWIRE. There are about 14 things there. I am sorry, Senator, but I was trying to write them down: yes on going to the private sector and keeping the program; yes on the court order for each search; and the last part was not that it—that it is useful to have the information from the program, roughly speaking?

Senator FEINSTEIN. Yes, for national security.

Mr. SWIRE. Yes, I agree with that also, yes.

Senator FEINSTEIN. Okay. Mr. Sunstein.

Mr. SUNSTEIN. I agree with every word.

Senator FEINSTEIN. Professor Stone.

Mr. STONE. I agree. I think it is important to understand what the value is. The value is not demonstrable from specific cases that have arisen in the past that suggest that but for 215 we would not have been able to thwart any particular terrorist attack. The value would be primarily—it is a needle in a haystack problem, that it is possible that in the future there will be an instance in which 215, if it exists, will enable us to prevent a major attack which otherwise we could not prevent. Our judgment was it does have value in that way.

Senator FEINSTEIN. Thank you.

Mr. Clarke, welcome. It is good to see you again. Yes or no?

Mr. CLARKE. Senator, I think we are, surprisingly, all in agreement.

Senator FEINSTEIN. Good. That is what I wanted to know. Thank you very much.

Now, the word "essential," this is a word that is debated as to its meaning. We have one recent court decision out of the Southern District of New York, and I would like to read from page 48 of that opinion. ''The effectiveness of bulk telephony metadata collection cannot be seriously disputed. Offering examples is a dangerous stratagem for the Government because it discloses means and methods of intelligence gathering. Such disclosures can only educate America's enemies. Nevertheless, the Government has acknowledged several successes in congressional testimony and in declarations that are part of the record in this case. In this court's view, they offer ample justification.'' And then it goes into al Qaeda-associated terrorists in Pakistan, connected with an unknown person in the United States, the Najibullah Zazi case, and particularly where 215, according to the court, came in was that NSA was able to provide a previously unknown number of one of the co-conspirators, Adis Medunjanin.

The next one is January 2009, an extremist in Yemen, a connection with Khalid Ozani in Texas, NSA notified the FBI, which discovered a nascent plot to attack the New York Stock Exchange. Using a 215 order, NSA queried telephony metadata to identify potential connections. Three defendants were convicted of terrorism offenses.

And the fourth—again, this is a court opinion—in October 2009, while monitoring an al Qaeda-affiliated terrorist, the NSA discovered David Headley, who is a major figure, was working on a plot to bomb a Danish newspaper office that had published cartoons depicting the prophet Muhammad. And it goes on from there.

So the word ''essential,'' I think is a word that is often debated. You also say that it was likely that with al-Mihdhar this could have prevented 9/11 and it could quite possibly prevent another 9/11. Am I correct about that, Mr. Morell?

Mr. MORELL. We as a group, ma'am, did not——

Senator FEINSTEIN. No. I am asking you what you said in the op-ed.

Mr. MORELL. Yes, I said that. But we never talked about that as a group, about 9/11. We never came to a judgment about that as a group.

Senator FEINSTEIN. Okay. So it was just your opinion.

Mr. MORELL. That was my opinion.

Senator FEINSTEIN. Now, let me ask you another. General Alexander testified to us that in 2009 the NSA did, in fact, go to the FISA Court and found that it took nine days average to be able to collect the information that was necessary. Are you aware of that?

Mr. MORELL. No, ma'am.

Senator FEINSTEIN. Well, that is according to testimony by General Alexander. We also know—my time is up? Is that what you are saying to me?

Chairman LEAHY. Yes. Go ahead and finish your question.

Senator FEINSTEIN. Would you just let me finish?

Chairman LEAHY. Of course.

Senator FEINSTEIN. I really appreciate that. Thank you.

He can be very strict.

This was used after the fact in the Boston bombing, but here is the difference: The Boston—and they used emergency powers, and they were able to get information quickly. This is used to prevent an attack. So those of us that see it important to prevent another attack—I do not need to tell you. Terrorism is up, groups have metastasized. We know they will come after us if they can. There is a real litany here of fact. So the question comes: Do you not find value, substantial value, in being able to prevent this attack?

Mr. MORELL. So I find substantial value in any tool that helps us prevent attacks. I believe that 215 carries the potential to prevent attacks, and that is why I think it needs to continue. But one of the important issues, I think, is the question of efficacy for us did not really impact our view on the change in approach to the program. We do not believe that we are going to add a substantial burden to the government by making the changes we are suggesting. If something cannot be done quicker than nine days, then they need to make some changes to make that happen.

We also wrote into our report an emergency provision so that in an emergency situation, when the intelligence community knows they need to move quickly, they will be able to query the data without a court order, going to the court after the fact.

Senator FEINSTEIN. Thank you very much.

Chairman LEAHY. And I should note—you were not here for this part of the testimony. When you talk about 9/11, one of the biggest problems there is that we had the information, it would have prevented 9/11. But the people with it did not communicate as they should have, and I recall some of the information we had finally being translated a week or two after the event.

Senator Lee.

Senator LEE. I am told that my distinguished colleague from South Carolina, a senior to me, needs to go somewhere, so in deference to the gentleman from South Carolina, I am going to let him go first.

Chairman LEAHY. Do you really want to give him that much deference?

Senator LEE. Well, he has been nice.

Chairman LEAHY. Can we vote on it?

Senator GRAHAM. I have always let you talk. And I think your air force base should be bigger.

[Laughter.]

Chairman LEAHY. Senator Graham, please go next.

Senator GRAHAM. Thank you.

Chairman LEAHY. And just so we will know, we will then go to Senator Blumenthal, then back to Senator Lee, then back to Senator Franken, then to Senator Cruz. Senator Graham.

Senator GRAHAM. Let us pick up on what the Chairman said. You wrote an op-ed——

Chairman LEAHY. And turn your microphone on.

Senator GRAHAM. Okay. There we go. Michael, you wrote an op-ed piece opining that you think that this technology, if it had been in place before 9/11, could have helped prevent the attack. That is your personal opinion.

Mr. MORELL. Yes, sir.

Senator GRAHAM. How many people agree with that? Raise your hand if you do.

Mr. SUNSTEIN. I would say, Senator, that——

Senator GRAHAM. That is not raising your hand.

Mr. SUNSTEIN. I think the reason we are not raising our hand is not that we disagree with Michael Morell, but that we are not specialists in the details of 9/11.

Senator GRAHAM. Fair enough.

Mr. SUNSTEIN. We did not investigate.

Senator FEINSTEIN. They said they did when I read it. They just said they did when I read it.

Senator GRAHAM. Well, we will just go with what you said.

Mr. SUNSTEIN. We agreed with the quotation Senator Feinstein read from Mr. Morell's *Washington Post* op-ed. On the 9/11 issue in particular, we did not discuss that as a group.

Senator GRAHAM. Okay. Well, we will take what she said. They agreed with you. That is good.

The bottom line is let us get way at the 30,000-foot level. What are we trying to do? Do you believe as a group we are at war with radical Islam?

Mr. MORELL. I do.

Senator GRAHAM. How many of you believe we are at war?

Mr. CLARKE. I think we all do, Senator.

Senator GRAHAM. Okay. The difference between fighting a crime and a war—there are fundamental differences. Do you agree with that? Intelligence gathering is a very important tool in fighting a war. Do you all agree with that?

Mr. SUNSTEIN. That is——

Senator GRAHAM. Prevention is important in crime——

Mr. SUNSTEIN. That is a theme of our report.

Senator GRAHAM. Yes, so I guess what I am trying to let the Nation know is that what you all gentlemen are trying to do is we are trying to find a way to fight a war within our values, and this is an unusual situation. There is no capital to conquer; there is no navy to sink; there is no air force to shoot down. We are fighting an ideology. And if we all believe that the enemy does not mind dying—as a matter of fact, that is first prize for these guys, is to die—we have got to hit them before they hit us. Is that generally the thought process here, we have got to identify the attack before it happens, they will not be deterred by death?

Mr. SUNSTEIN. That sounds fair, and some version of that is in our report.

Senator GRAHAM. Okay. Fair enough. Now, Anwar al-Awlaki, he is deceased, but he was an American citizen in Yemen. How did we miss the fact that a major in the United States Army was communicating with him? I mean, we have got all these programs, and everybody is wanting to revisit these programs, which I totally understand. But we have got a major in the United States Army that wound up killing 199 people, I think, that was openly talking for the whole world to see to one of the chief terrorist suspects in the world in Yemen. How did we miss that? And what can we do to make sure we do not miss that in the future?

Mr. STONE. I do not quite understand, to be honest, the thrust of the question. I mean, our recommendations do not take away the ability of the government to use the bulk telephony metadata program. We shift where it stays, whether that is from the government or to private sources. We say a court order should be necessary. But as we made very clear in the report, we do believe it is critical to protect the national security of the United States, and we believe that our recommendations are consistent——

Senator GRAHAM. The fact that nobody can answer the question—I understand reforming the program and trying to be more sensitive to privacy concerns. But no one has really talked much about the fact that you had a major in the United States Army on active duty openly communicating with a known terrorist, following his every word, and eventually got radicalized and killed 19——

Mr. SWIRE. Senator, if I—so we do have a section in the report about military and war that talks about how the same Internet, the same hardware, the same software that is used in Afghanistan and Iraq these days are used back home. And so when it comes to the surveillance on hardware and software over there, it is the same hardware and software here. And that did not used to be true to nearly the same extent in previous wars. So how we build an Internet at home and an Internet for warfighting is a challenge we talk about in the report.

Senator GRAHAM. Let us just use the Anwar al-Awlaki analogy. If he is calling someone—we got his cell phone, and he is dialing someone in the United States, calling someone, the program after the changes you are recommending, can it still pick that up?

Mr. SWIRE. Yes.

Mr. MORELL. Yes.

Senator GRAHAM. Okay. Would a court order be necessary?

Mr. CLARKE. Unless there was an emergency, yes.

Senator GRAHAM. Well, do you agree with me that you do not need a court order to surveil the enemy in a time of war?

Mr. CLARKE. Overseas, yes.

Mr. SUNSTEIN. Not in the United States.

Senator GRAHAM. Do you agree with me he would be an enemy combatant, that he would fit the definition of an ''enemy combatant''?

Mr. SUNSTEIN. We would probably want to look at that, you know, the legal authorities on that. I do not think we disagree with it, but the point of a legal view——

Senator GRAHAM. Well, the main point is that you believe we can still pick up that phone call?

Mr. SUNSTEIN. Okay. Well, we—yes, we distinguish——

Senator GRAHAM. Okay. That is all I wanted. That is good.

Now, if somebody is calling him from the United States, can we pick up that phone call and do something about it?

Mr. SWIRE. If either end is overseas, it is not 215 that is an issue. It is 702 or the Executive order.

Senator GRAHAM. Most Americans could care less about the titles. They just want to know if somebody in the——

Mr. SWIRE. But it is relevant to our recommendations, sir, because on 702, which is the one side is overseas, we keep the same structure basically it has today, and we are not——

Senator GRAHAM. Okay. So can you reassure America that if somebody in the United States is calling a known terrorist in Yemen, we can pick that up and do something about it?

Mr. CLARKE. Yes.

Senator GRAHAM. And at the end of the day—my time is up—isn't that what we are trying to do? Aren't we trying to find out who is talking to who when the person, one of the people doing the talking is somebody we are really worried about attacking the Nation, and we are really not trying to do anything more than that?

Mr. SUNSTEIN. Yes, Senator, and I think that is a very important point because it applies both domestically, where there are concerns about monitoring of American citizens that do not fit our aims, and also internationally, where our focus is on the source of situations you are discussing and not on picking up people's private communications.

Senator GRAHAM. Thank you all for your service to our country.

Chairman LEAHY. And I appreciate you knowing the difference between the 702 and the 215, of course, and I would say to my friend, Senator Graham, we have to look at what are adequate safeguards, especially when we are dealing with an agency that did not have adequate enough safeguards to keep a subcontractor from stealing millions and millions and millions of files and he is still out today after spending millions of dollars, do not know all that he did steal. And I just do not want to get lured by all the technology we have, lured into complacency. We saw the same thing—and I do not mean to be picking on just the NSA, when the State Department and the military put all kinds of files where a private first class could go in and download it all on a Lady Gaga CD and then cause, as we all know, enormous difficulties for the United States when these highly classified cables from our Ambassadors were made public.

Senator Blumenthal.

Senator BLUMENTHAL. Thank you, Mr. Chairman. Thank you for holding this hearing. Thank you to each of you for your very impressive and extraordinarily important work. I think you have elevated and provided credibility to a very specific and very significant proposal that advanced the reform effort in our intelligence-gathering operations. And, you know, Senator Graham referred to the present effort to counter terrorism as a "war." There is a saying—it is an adage. I believe it is attributed to the Romans. My classic education is not good enough to know. But the saying is, "In war, law is the first casualty." And you have provided a really profoundly important service in making sure that we do not have law as the casualty. And as you say in your report—it is the first principle you state—"The U.S. Government must protect at once two different forms of security: national security and personal privacy." And there is a reason why courts matter, why the Founders of our Nation thought they mattered. They wanted to prevent general warrants and secret courts, like the Star Chamber. And it was one of the reasons they rebelled against it.

And so my questions focus on the Court, and I have advanced and proposed the constitutional advocate, the public interest advocate, however you want to label it, that would be independence, institutionalized to assure that there is an adversarial proceeding whenever the advocate thought it was necessary, not on an ad hoc basis, not when the Court thought it might be useful. But courts benefit from hearing both sides and from having the advocate decide that another side should be represented.

And I would like to hear from you, because we have heard the contrary point of view that it should be an amicus brief, as it has been sometimes called, or some other kind of ad hoc proceeding, and maybe beginning, Professor Sunstein, with you, stating on behalf of the panel why you chose this structure, because obviously the President is going to have to make a decision as to whether to adopt that idea, and we as a panel and the Senate will have to deliberate as well.

Mr. SUNSTEIN. Well, history is relevant here. There was an understanding when the Court was created that it would be basically dealing with issues of fact, like whether a warrant was justified, not with large issues of law and policy. And as the system has developed over the years, as you are well aware, Senator, often the judges are being asked to decide those large questions. And so an adversary proceeding seems warranted in a setting of that kind.

We are well aware that some judges for whom we have a lot of admiration on the Court believe that the judge ought to be in charge of deciding when the public interest advocate is relevant.

We think that is not consistent with our traditions. Normally it is not the case that the judge gets to decide this interest gets a lawyer. So we think to have someone who is a dedicated officer designed to protect privacy and liberty interests is a very important safeguard.

Senator BLUMENTHAL. And the provision of an adversarial proceeding such as you have described, which reflects the change in the role of the Court—I think that is a very important point—would not necessarily delay it or imperil security if there were preclearance and if warrants were granted and then reviewed afterward. In other words, we all know in the ordinary criminal process some of us have knocked on a judge's door literally in the middle of the night if we thought it was necessary to get a warrant. And the same principle applies here, does it not?

Mr. SUNSTEIN. Yes, that is very important. So Senator Feinstein and Senator Graham rightly draw attention to the immediacy of certain threats, the fact that something is coming in a way where you need information fast, and as you say, it is consistent with our traditions to accommodate emergency situations.

Senator BLUMENTHAL. And in the short time I have remaining, perhaps I could ask you to elaborate a little bit on the reasons why you recommended a change in the method of selection, which I agree is very, very important to the trust and confidence in this process. And I think one of the reasons for reforming the whole system is to preserve and enhance trust and confidence of the American people that we are doing both forms of security here, national security and personal privacy.

Mr. SUNSTEIN. Yes, I think it was Justice Frankfurter—I may have the reference wrong—who emphasized both the importance of doing justice and the appearance that justice is done, and that is connected with your point.

We also think, particularly in the context of the selection of the judges for the FISA Court, a little diversity is a good idea across Democratic and Republican appointees. And as the report makes clear, we have all the respect in the world for the Chief Justice and have, you know, nothing critical to say about him in this connection. But it just is the case that if 10 of 11 come from one political party in terms of the appointing President, that is awkward, and so we would like to see some more diversity.

Senator BLUMENTHAL. And, again, it is in accord with the traditions of our judicial system that appearance and perception has to be served because of the immense and in many respects undemocratic powers that courts exert, undemocratic because we believe in elections generally, and here we have unelected FISA Court members operating in secret or other members of the judiciary operating in the open, but they too are unelected.

And so I think that your point is very, very important, and I again thank you all for your service to our Nation.

Thank you.

Senator FEINSTEIN [presiding]. Thank you very much, Senator Blumenthal.

The Chairman of this Committee has asked that we recess for five minutes, and so without objection, we will recess for five minutes.

[Recess at 3:30 p.m. to 3:37 p.m.]

Senator LEE [presiding]. It is rare that a freshman from the minority party gets to chair a Committee proceeding like this one, but, you know, who says the race goeth not to the swift?

First of all, I really appreciate all of you coming here, and I appreciate your willingness to serve on the President's Review Group. The work that you have done has been very helpful, and I am confident that it will do a lot to frame this important discussion as we move forward.

The importance of these issues cannot be overstated. One of the things that I liked that you pointed out in your report appears on page 15 wherein you pointed out an interesting coincidence, you might call it—my word, not yours—that the concept of security has dual meaning. On the one hand, it refers to the fact that one of the most important, fundamental, sacred obligations of government is to keep the people safe, to protect us from each other and to protect us from those outside of our country who would harm us. Security is one of the most important functions that the Federal Government has. And at the very same time, it refers to something different, it refers to something else that might appear to be in conflict with to create tension with that first concept, and that is the concept of security referred to in the Fourth Amendment, that we have the right under the Fourth Amendment to be secure, to be secure in our persons, houses, papers, and effects against unreasonable searches and seizures.

Now, this concept of what that means to be secure in this second respect has, of course, changed over time. It has necessary changed as our technology has changed. But the fundamental principles underlying that concept of security must necessarily remain the same in order for us to remain a free society and in order for our constitutional protections to continue to be meaningful.

One of the things that we have struggled with as a Congress and that we struggle with really as a country as a whole relates to the fact that where we keep our papers and what our papers are has changed, especially in the last few years. No longer do our papers consist exclusively of actual paper. What the founding generation would have thought of as papers often exists only in the ether, exists only in the electronic equivalence of ones and zeros. And those are not any longer stored exclusively on hard drives with a finite location that might be in our home. A lot of the time they exist only in a cloud somewhere. And yet these pieces of information, these papers or effects or whatever you want to call them, in many instances are things in which we have, or at least reasonably should have, an expectation of privacy that is reasonable, to say the very least.

And so we have to figure out how best to balance these two sometimes conflicting interests associated with security. There are several ways in which this arises, but we have talked a little bit today about the collection of metadata and the fact that we have got an enormous amount of metadata that has been collected on potentially 300 million Americans.

The government notes that it has in place a rigorous review process that must be followed before anyone accesses this data base containing metadata on basically every American. What concerns me about that is the fact that these are basically internal operating procedures. And so what is a policy today, which may well be followed religiously for all I know today, could change tomorrow. And I am willing to assume, for purposes of this discussion, that the men and women who work at the NSA have nothing but our best interests at heart. I am willing to assume that, at least for purposes of this discussion. That might not be the case a year from now or four years from now or 10 years from now or 40 years from now.

In fact, we have seen this movie before. We know how it ends. We know that eventually, if that much information remains in the hands of government for that long, it will eventually be abused. It will be manipulated for partisan and otherwise nefarious purposes. And we cannot let that happen.

So let us start with Professor Stone. When we look at this, would this be something that you would describe a one of the most compelling arguments in favor of putting more robust restrictions in law so that they are not simply in the hands of people, however well intentioned they might be, within the NSA?

Mr. STONE. Yes, I think this is—our primary concern with respect to the collection of metadata is not the actual use of the metadata in the ways in which it is authorized, but the risk that somewhere down the road, someone will figure out how to and want to misuse that data. And so we think safeguards are critical.

I should also say I think the safeguards that are now in place internally are actually quite good. And they are rigorous, they are multifaceted. There are checks and balances. There are the Senate and House Intelligence Committees. There are Inspectors General, there is the Attorney General, the FISA Court. All are looking over this.

But even so, our judgment is that it should be taken out of the hands of the government in terms of the holding of the data, and that reduces—it does not eliminate entirely but reduces substantially, we think, the potential for the data to be abused in the ways that you are talking about. And it is still a question of tradeoffs, because even there, there is always a risk. But our judgment is that is an important step toward reducing the risk on one side, while at the same time preserving the value of the data for national security purposes.

Senator LEE. I think that is right, and for that reason, Chairman Leahy and I and several of my other colleagues across the aisle have introduced legislation to try to reform this process in one form or another.

If I can ask one follow-up on this, an additional follow-up on this, Mr. Chairman? Some have suggested that it would simply be infeasible, categorically infeasible ever to require a court order as a condition precedent for performing a query of the government data base. And let us assume, for purposes of this discussion, that the data set will remain—at least does remain for the time being in the possession of the government and that we are not going to move to a different system in which the government does not have possession.

The argument frequently arises. You cannot possibly require any kind of a court order as a condition precedent for querying that data base, even where you have got U.S. citizens involved in the query because it would just take too much time.

Do you know of any reason why that should necessarily be the case or why that would unavoidably be the case, why we could not get around that by perhaps creating additional FISA Court positions?

Mr. STONE. We find that wholly unconvincing. Our view is that there are practical realities about it. If you are going to add the burdens to the FISA Court, you have got to add resources, you have got to add judges or magistrate judges, if necessary; but that there is no reason why the argument about getting a court order for a query of the metadata is any more impossible than it is to get a search warrant to search a home. Fundamentally, this is what we do all the time, and there are great protections in having judges oversee this, and there is no good reason why this should not be adopted in this context as well.

Senator LEE. Thank you. Thank you, Professor.

Thank you, Chairman.

Chairman LEAHY [presiding]. Thank you, Senator Lee.

Senator Franken.

Senator FRANKEN. Thank you, Mr. Chairman, and thank you, gentlemen, for this report. I think it will be a real help as we work to improve our privacy and surveillance laws.

On page 124 of your report, you wrote, ''A free people can govern themselves only if they have access to the information that they need to make wise judgments about public policy.'' I could not agree with you more, and right now the American people do not have the information that they need to make up their own minds about these programs.

I have a bipartisan bill that would fix this, the *Surveillance Transparency Act of 2013*. It has the support of 14 of my colleagues and the strong support of the business community, which has broadly endorsed the principle of transparency and has endorsed my bill specifically.

When we met last year, late last year, when I submitted written comments to your group, I urged you to support the reforms in my bill, and I am pleased that your report endorses the same measures that are at the core of my bill. I am going to focus my questions on the transparency reforms that we agree on.

First, my question is on government transparency. Seven months after the Snowden leaks, the government has yet to publicly disclose even a rough estimate of how many people have had their information collected in the telephone metadata or PRISM programs. This is not an accident. Under current law, the American government does not have to do this.

My bill would force the government to annually disclose an estimate of the number of people who have had their information collected by the NSA under each key surveillance authority. Your report supports this.

You say that for key surveillance authorities, "the government should, to the greatest extent possible, report publicly on the total number of requests made and the number of individuals whose records have been requested."

Why did you support this particular transparency reform? Mr. Sunstein, why don't you begin, and whoever else wants to comment, do so.

Mr. SUNSTEIN. Well, a theme of our report, consistent with your bill, is that sunlight is the best of disinfectants, as Justice Brandeis said, and that it is very important for the American people, unless there is a very strong national security justification on the other side, to get a sense of what their government is doing. So the first and foremost goal is about democratic self-government and a free society. That is one of the things that distinguishes our Nation from some others. And another idea to which you also referred has to do with economic interests, which should not be trivialized; that there are American companies who are at economic risk because it is thought that the American government is forcing them to turn over all sorts of stuff. It is just not true. Sunlight shows that the program is much narrower and targeted than some people fear.

Senator FRANKEN. And my bill does that, and I want to talk about that next. But any other comments on that?

I am going to just continue to drill down on this first recommendation because it is different from what the administration has been saying and is saying. Your report calls for the government to say how many people have had their information collected. My bill calls for the government to say how many people have had their information collected. Yet last November, representatives from the Office of the Director of National Intelligence and the NSA came before the Subcommittee on Privacy, Technology, and the Law, which I chair, and testified that it would be "difficult, if not impossible" for the government to say how many people have had their information collected under these authorities.

Mr. Swire, did the administration communicate this concern to you? If so, why did you find it unpersuasive?

Mr. SWIRE. Thank you, Senator. We talked in some detail with the administration about transparency provisions. They certainly expressed concern at when there is a provider that has a very small number of customers, for instance, that we not tip off people who is being surveilled in those cases. There is a national security problem there.

I think when it comes to the number of people who have been touched by the orders, they did not focus in their discussions with us on that risk in transparency. And my own sense, having talked, among others, with the companies on this, is that if there are cooperative efforts to have the companies, the providers, work with the government, that we are likely to be able to come up with practices that allow estimates. You might not have exact numbers in all cases because sometimes you do not know if the same email applies to three people or one person. So with precision, you might not have exact details, but I think you can have good trend numbers and you can have a good overall sense of what is happening.

Senator FRANKEN [presiding]. Well, I am out of my time, and as you can see, we have another vote, so we will recess for five minutes for another vote. Before we do, I just want to, Mr. Sunstein, just reiterate this thing about the companies, their ability to disclose because it is hurting them. And we had an analytics firm, Forrester, say that the American cloud computing industry stands to lose up to $180 billion by 2016 as a result of increased distrust of their services, particularly abroad. So thank you for that being part of your recommendation.

We will recess for five minutes because I have got to go vote, and I better go right now. So we are recessed—oh, Senator Cruz, good, good. I am sorry. I guess I am the Chair.

[Laughter.]

Senator FRANKEN. I call on Senator Cruz.

Senator CRUZ. Thank you, Senator Franken. And I want to begin by just thanking each of the members of the panel, thanking you for your service in the intelligence community and thank you for your service looking at the difficult and important legal issues and privacy issues that surround this critical area.

I think a great many Americans have concerns about the current state of NSA surveillance. I, for one, have concerns on two different fronts. I am concerned, on the one hand, that the Federal Government has not been effective enough monitoring and surveilling bad guys, that we have not succeeded in preventing what should have been preventable terrorist attacks. And at the same time, I am concerned that the sweep of the surveillance has been far too broad with respect to law-abiding citizens. And I think a great many Americans would prefer to see that reversed—far greater scrutiny on bad guys, people that we have reason to suspect may be planning a terrorist attack, and far more protection for law-abiding citizens who have committed no transgressions.

And so I want to begin on the first piece, on targeting bad guys, and I want to follow up with the question Senator Graham asked earlier concerning Major Hasan and his communications with al-Awlaki, a known terrorist leader. Despite all of our surveillance capabilities, despite having significant indications that Major Hasan was engaged in these communications, the Federal Government failed to prevent the horrific terrorist attack that claimed the lives of 14 innocents at Fort Hood.

And so the first question I would like to ask the panel is: In your judgment, why is that? What was lacking that prevented us from acquiring the information and acting on it to prevent that act of terror?

Mr. SUNSTEIN. Well, I guess I would say that it is a very important question, and your general thought that to target through surveillance of known bad guys, that is something that we did devote a great deal of attention to, and Recommendation 15 is, I would say, of great importance. It has gotten essentially no attention so far as I can tell. Not even on Twitter has it gotten attention. And that recommendation is that we need to expand our authority to track known targets of counterterrorism when they first enter the United States. So that is a gap in our statutory structure, that when they come to the United States they get protections immediately so we cannot track them.

Whether that would apply in any way to the case you are describing I just—I do not think so, but it is an important gap. That one, I think probably as a group, we would need to get more into the details than we did.

Senator CRUZ. Mr. Morell, I would welcome your thoughts also on how we could have done better preventing that terrorist attack.

Mr. MORELL. Senator, it is not something that we as a group looked at. That was not our mandate. I am familiar with the case, obviously. I am a little constrained here because I do not know what is in the unclassified world and what is in the classified world. So maybe we could have a conversation afterward in closed session.

Senator CRUZ. Okay. A follow-up question for the panel if anyone would care to comment. The same is true with respect to the Tsarnaev brothers, the Boston bombers, where in that instance we had intelligence from Russia that they were having communications with radical Islamic groups, and yet for whatever reason their radicalization continued, the government dropped the ball, and they carried out yet another horrific terrorist attack.

Do members of the panel have any views as to why our surveillance capability did not provide sufficient information to act upon to prevent that terrorist attack before it occurred?

Mr. MORELL. So, Senator, I will tell you, in that case there were not any communications between the United States and overseas, so there was no surveillance of those communications that would have provided any information that would have prevented the Boston bombings. And this is largely a case of domestic radicalization, and I think that is the best way to think about it.

Senator CRUZ. Well, as I understand it, the elder Tsarnaev brother, after traveling to Chechnya, after meeting with radical Islamic groups, came back and posted on public YouTube pages admonitions to jihad. And that certainly does not take extraordinary surveillance capability. It simply takes the government looking to what he is saying publicly and loudly before that terrorist attack is carried out.

Mr. MORELL. Yes, and I was making a different point, Senator. You are absolutely right, but I was making a different point about actual communications and the collection of those communications.

Senator CRUZ. Well, and I think that underscores that my concern that the focus of the programs has been far too much on law-abiding citizens and far too little on people for whom we have significant reason to believe there may be a real danger of terrorism. And with respect to Major Hasan, with respect to the Tsarnaev brothers, I am not sure there could have been too much surveillance based on the information we had to protect national security.

Now, flipping to citizens at large, am I understanding correctly the conclusions that the commission received that, in your judgment, the bulk metadata program has not to date prevented any specific terrorist attack? Is that an accurate understanding?

Mr. STONE. Yes, that is a fair understanding. We think that it has contributed some useful information, but could not say that any particular terrorist attack has been prevented because of the information learned from the metadata program.

Senator CRUZ. Now, an additional recommendation, as I understand it from the commission, is that the government itself stopped collecting metadata, but that private companies, the phone companies that already have that data preserve that data, and that searches be conducted only when there is specific cause to search rather than in a blanket sense the government sweeping in every law-abiding citizen.

Mr. STONE. Precisely.

Senator CRUZ. And is it the judgment of the commission that if the data were kept in private hands of the phone companies that already possess the data legally, that that would do nothing to undermine the efficacy of the program preventing potentially future attacks?

Mr. STONE. We believe that that way of handling the data can be done in a way that would not in any way undermine the efficacy of the program. On the other hand, we recognize in our report that that is speculative. We do not know that for a fact. And if, in fact, it turns out that there are inefficiencies that make it more difficult to use the data in an appropriate way, that the alternative is to have it held by a single private holder. And that would basically eliminate most of the inefficiencies.

Senator CRUZ. Focusing also on the question of potentially overbroad surveillance, a couple of weeks ago Senator Sanders wrote a letter to the NSA asking if the NSA, quote, has spied or is the NSA currently spying on Members of Congress or other American elected officials, and the NSA's response to that was Members of Congress have the same privacy protections as all U.S. persons, which certainly suggests the answer to that question is in the affirmative.

Now, as I understand it, each of you were granted security clearances and the ability to see classified information and court opinions. So the question I would ask this panel is: Are you aware, has the NSA ever done surveillance on Members of Congress or other elected American officials?

Mr. SUNSTEIN. We are not aware of any such, and one of the things we learned in our review is that there is no targeting by the NSA of people because of their political views or their religious convictions or their political party. So in terms of concretely some details, we may not have precise questions that every one of which we have off-the-top-of-the-mind answers to, but politics, religion, political views, that is not what they are interested in.

Mr. SWIRE. Just one small thing. We are talking about in recent years. We are not talking about back in the 1960s and 1970s when there was a different history about intelligence agencies doing things that got exposed.

Senator CRUZ. No, I mean in current years, although I do want to clarify, Professor Sunstein, one thing you said about religious views. I assume you would agree that a commitment to jihad would not qualify as a religious view and, indeed, would be a political position and embrace of violence that merits very close scrutiny to prevent that violence from being carried out.

Mr. SUNSTEIN. Yes, if there is reason to believe the person is threatening to the United States, that would not fall within protected religious belief.

Senator CRUZ. A follow-up question related to the question about Members of Congress. Is any member of the panel aware whether the NSA has spied or is spying on the judiciary or, in particular, members of the Supreme Court?

Mr. SUNSTEIN. We have no information to that effect and would not anticipate that.

Senator CRUZ. Very good. Well, I want to thank each of you for being here. The remainder of the Committee is off voting, and so with that, we will take a five-minute recess. And then I expect my colleagues will return, and the hearing will commence again then. Thank you.

[Recess at 4:05 p.m. to 4:15 p.m.]

Chairman LEAHY [presiding]. I am almost afraid to ask what the joke is, but those hidden microphones we have under your table probably will tell us. The surveillance camera.

[Laughter.]

Chairman LEAHY. People are coming back. I just wanted to note a couple quotes from your report. One is the question is not whether granting the government authority makes us incrementally safer, but whether the additional safety is worth the sacrifice in terms of individual privacy, personal liberty, and public trust. It is the public trust, as we know—you know, so many times we have to rely on individuals in the public who might give us information that can be valuable, but they have to have the public trust. Law enforcement knows this, the same with the intelligence community. And I think I am about to yield to Senator Whitehouse but, Mr. Morell, in your review did you identify a difference—and I think you have already answered this in one question—between the demonstrated utility of the government's activities under Section 702 of FISA, which is aimed at non-U.S. persons abroad, and that of the phone records program under Section 215?

Mr. MORELL. Yes, Mr. Chairman. 702 has proven to be much, much more valuable as a counterterrorism tool than has 215.

Chairman LEAHY. Thank you very much.

Senator Whitehouse.

Senator WHITEHOUSE. Thank you, Chairman.

Mr. Morell, how would you characterize the value of the 215 program from an intelligence perspective and, if you will, from a safety perspective? Even if it has not generated intelligence, the fact that it could might be of some value, and I am interested in your assessment of its value in both of those dimensions.

Mr. MORELL. Yes, Senator, that is exactly where I am. It is absolutely true that 215 has not, by itself, disrupted, prevented terrorist attacks in the United States. But that does not mean that it is not important going forward, because as I said in my op-ed, it only needs to be successful once to be invaluable.

One of the ways that I think about this is many of us have never suffered a fire in our homes, but we still all have homeowners' insurance to protect against that. And that is one of the ways I think about 215.

Senator WHITEHOUSE. I have had the concern that the prospect of an unauthorized leak and a sudden, spontaneous, unanticipated disclosure was not foreseen by the intelligence community, and that there did not appear to be a response that was timely, sensible, where it did not seem to be at all prepared. What is your sense of what the reaction was by the intelligence community? Was it really as much of a scramble as it looked like from the outside?

Mr. MORELL. Senator, I was inside for part of it and outside for part of it. So my sense is that the strategy that was being pursued was not successful, clearly not successful. The strategy that was pursued did not deal—did not mitigate the lack of public trust, did not win back any of the public trust.

It was absolutely clear to me—and this picks up on something Professor Stone raised earlier—that this was, as you know, one of the most overseen programs in the history of the intelligence community, within NSA——

Senator WHITEHOUSE. In the history of the country, I would say.

Mr. MORELL. In the history of the country. Within NSA, within the executive branch and the interagency, within the Justice Department, within the Intelligence Committees of Congress, and with the judiciary, which is, as you know, very, very unusual for an intelligence program. And I think that there was a sense in the intelligence agencies and in the executive branch that that level of oversight was enough to keep the public trust if there was a disclosure, and I think that turned out to be wrong.

Senator WHITEHOUSE. I wonder if it might have done better if within the first couple of weeks, frankly, a full disclosure of how the program had been carefully overseen came out, because it took, it seemed to me, days initially and really weeks until there was a solid, comprehensive review. In fact, what you have just said is one of the clearer expositions that we have heard yet. I think this is one of those cases where, you know, a not completely accurate image got across town before the truth got its boots on, and this is going to happen again. I mean, we live in a society in which there are going to be leaks. And I think for the intelligence community not to be prepared for this is a mistake, and in particular, it is a mistake because there was no analysis of—if it all happens at once and we make a hash of responding to it, what happens to this program, you dial back from that, if that is the way you are thinking, to being more candid up front and diminishing that risk. And I think we could have been a lot more candid with the American people up front about this program without creating any significant national security loss.

So, anyway, that is my thought. My time is running out, and I just want to take a moment and thank you for your service to our country. In my time on the Intelligence Committee, I found you always extremely capable and honorable. And I want to also thank

Mr. Clarke here, who has warned of many things that, if we and others had listened more carefully, we could have avoided some real disasters. So I am very pleased that both of you are here today and want to thank you.

Chairman LEAHY. As Chairman of this Committee, I would join with that.

What we are going to do, I am going to yield to Senator Sessions, who has been running back and forth with me to vote. I am going to ask Senator Blumenthal, the senior Senator from Connecticut, to take the Chair. Then we will recognize Senator Coons and Senator Klobuchar. But before I leave, with the indulgence of the Members, I have spent decades on this Committee. We have had some terrific panels. I cannot think of anybody that brings the wealth and broadness of knowledge to an issue that the five of you do. And I say that just because you have given a great deal of your time to public service, but a great deal of your time in doing this, and it is extremely valuable. Whatever we do is going to be influenced heavily by your report, and I appreciate that. I know the President also appreciates the amount of time you have done. With some of you I go back longer, as I have with Mr. Clarke, but, Mr. Morell, in your days especially as Acting Director of the CIA, the clearness of the briefings you gave to several of us—it was unfortunate they were all closed-door so the public did not see that they were, but they were extraordinarily helpful, and that was something you heard from both Republicans and Democrats, and I appreciate that.

And, of course, Professor Sunstein and I have know each other for a long, long time, and he has been extremely helpful to this Committee.

Professor Stone, Professor Swire, thank you so much for the time you have taken.

So I am going to turn it over to Senator Blumenthal and yield to Senator Sessions.

Senator SESSIONS. Thank you. Well, I know Senator Leahy has spent a number of years dealing with these issues also, and I believe the *PATRIOT Act* that he helped craft and we all worked on and spent hours and hours and hours on was not one of these things where you have to reduce constitutional rights in order to protect America. I think that was the wrong characterization of it. I believe everything in that bill was consistent with then-existing criminal law techniques that were used every day by prosecutors in the counties of America, in the U.S. Attorney's Offices, which I was for almost 15 years. And I do not believe that there is anything there that we should be apologizing for.

So the committee is an excellent committee and a highly intelligent committee, but I would note that three of the members never had hands-on experience with this. You have written about it, but you have not been in the field directly dealing with these issues. And I think anyone would say it is a pro-civil libertarian panel; therefore, I am rather pleased that you fundamentally, I think, agreed with at least some of what I have said.

You say, " ... although recent disclosures and commentary have created the impression in some quarters that NSA surveillance is indiscriminate and pervasive across the globe, that is not the case.

NSA focuses on collecting foreign intelligence information that is relevant to protecting the national security of the United States and its allies.'' And I think that—I know you did not say that lightly. I know you would not have said that if you did not believe it.

You go on to say the group ''found no evidence of illegality or other abuse of authority for the purpose of targeting domestic political activity.'' I think that is good to hear, and that has always been my impression.

And, also, you said, ''In our review, we have not uncovered any official efforts to suppress dissent or any intent to intrude into people's private lives without legal justification. NSA is interested in protecting the national security, not in personal details unrelated to that concern.''

Of the 300-and-something million American people, they are not interested in what all we are saying on our telephone calls. So I think that is important. I thank you for that. And I believe those who have raised concerns about it could take comfort, some comfort into that.

I was a prosecutor, as I said, for a long time, and I want to raise a question about the metadata. That sounds so awful and scary that it makes us nervous, but in conventional prosecutions in America today, a county prosecutor who is interested in knowing who a criminal suspect is talking to issues a subpoena to the phone company, and they submit the records to him. And then he examines the records to see if Bad Guy One is talking to Bad Guy Two shortly before the robbery took place, or whatever. This is the kind of thing that is done every day in every office.

The DEA, the IRS can issue records—obtain your motel records, your telephone records. The IRS can get every bank record you have administratively—they do not even have to issue a grand jury subpoena for it—and examine somebody's financial records.

Now, the reason is these are not their records. They are not the individual who is being investigated records. They are the phone companies' records, the bank records, the hotel's records. Right? I mean, that is the difference. You have a diminished expectation of privacy, the Supreme Court has clearly held for the last 100 years, I suppose, in records not held by you.

Okay. So the records now are brought to the United States somehow. They are in our custody because of the way the computer systems work, and we get numbers, basically. So, Mr. Morell, I guess you have used this system. Would you share with us, is there any difference between the traditional issuing of subpoenas for records and the way this is done and what the importance, or lack of it, of the government getting the records from the companies in bulk and then accessing them? And, finally, to what extent is content obtained, the actual conversations?

Mr. MORELL. Yes, Senator, I am not the best person to answer that question, so let me defer to my colleagues.

Senator SESSIONS. Okay. Who would like to—Mr. Stone? And, Mr. Stone, I am glad to hear your comment, but you are on the board at the ACLU, I believe. Is that right?

Mr. STONE. The National Advisory Board, yes.

Senator SESSIONS. And did you support the ACLU lawsuit against the government raising many issues concerning this?

Mr. STONE. I had nothing whatever to do with that at all.

Senator SESSIONS. So you do not feel any conflict——

Mr. STONE. No.

Senator SESSIONS [continuing]. In serving on this—Okay.

Mr. STONE. Not in this way.

Senator SESSIONS. Go ahead and see if you could—I would be glad to hear your answer.

Mr. STONE. I think what has changed is the nature of the technology, and so when you talk about subpoenas, whether it is through a grand jury or an administrative subpoena, typically they are looking for very focused type of information relevant to a particular investigation, narrowly defined.

When you are comparing this to the metadata, you are talking about millions of Americans' records swept up. No subpoena——

Senator SESSIONS. Now, wait a minute. "Swept up." It is somewhere in a computer.

Mr. STONE. No subpoena has ever been allowed to reach that breadth that happens under the metadata program. So I think the analogy is simply a flawed analogy.

Senator SESSIONS. Well, nobody is going through and looking at every record that is there. They have to have some sort of indicia that is valuable on investigation to even inquire into it.

Mr. STONE. Yes, but you were drawing an analogy to the subpoena, and what I am saying is that the subpoena traditionally has to be relatively narrowly drawn to particular information directly relevant to a particular inquiry. And the metadata program does, in fact, elicit vast amounts of data far beyond anything that any subpoena in the history of the world has been allowed to gather.

Senator SESSIONS. Well, okay. Let us get this straight. So the metadata comes in, and the only difference is it was in the computers of the phone company, but for easier access, it is put in the computer of the government somewhere. And the inquiries only go to those records, just like they would have gone to the phone company. The only difference is for convenience in computer access, the government can get it quicker because some of these issues are life and death.

Mr. STONE. As the Supreme Court—five Justices, at least, of the Supreme Court have explicitly recognized a year ago, there are limits that technology now has called into play about how far this doctrine that, if you disclose information to somebody else, that you have no reasonable expectation of privacy in the information. So in the Jones case, five Justices, including Justice Alito, in a very important opinion, suggested that that basic principle that, as you say, was around for a long time has to be called into question when you get into a world where technology allows——

Senator SESSIONS. Well, they have not held that to this date, have they?

Mr. STONE. Excuse me?

Senator SESSIONS. You say they called into question. No holding has been so held.

Mr. STONE. No, and there would be nothing we say has anything to do with——

Senator SESSIONS. I do not see why they would hold that. I do not see any difference really. You are accessing the same records whether you get them from the phone company or whether in bulk in a more accessible account.

Mr. SUNSTEIN. Senator, if this is helpful, I think the direction you are going in is actually quite compatible with our recommendation. So our recommendation is not that we eliminate the 215 program but that we have a program where the government does not have all this stuff, which the government does not in the cases you worked on as a prosecutor or district attorney. It does not just have it. It gets access to it on a certain showing. And that is exactly the model that we are suggesting, and what we suggest is that that model will not compromise any national security goal because in cases where time is of the essence, human life is on the line, you can get at it like that; and because in cases where it is not on the line, you go through the standard legal process.

So the analogy from tradition, to which you have rightly referred, that is actually what we are building on in our recommendation.

Senator SESSIONS. My time is up. Thank you. General Mukasey, former Attorney General Mukasey, a federal judge for 20 years, does not agree—he thinks that will impact adversely, the mechanism of the system—in a recent op-ed.

Thank you.

Senator BLUMENTHAL [presiding]. Thank you, Senator Sessions. Senator Coons.

Senator COONS. Thank you, Senator Blumenthal, and I would like to thank the entire panel for your service to our Nation, for your testimony here today, and for your hard work to make sure that we really focus on and get right some of these tough questions.

Just to follow up on the exchange that just happened, if you might, Professor Swire, how did the Review Group's suggestions surrounding the Section 215 authority address the constitutional concerns that were raised by Judge Lee? And if you could just focus us on the outcomes.

Mr. SWIRE. Thank you, Senator. Our task that we were asked to do was not focused on Constitutional analysis. Our task was on what policy should be going forward. So as a group, we did not try to make an assessment on the constitutional issue.

Senator COONS. But in your view, do the group's recommendations actually address some of those concerns or fail to address them?

Mr. SWIRE. Well, we tried to do the task we were assigned. I think that as Professor Stone was just saying, there is discussion in the report about how metadata looks given changing technology. And so in the 1970s, there were a limited number of phone calls. Today the number of texts and Facebook posts and everything is enormously different, and that kind of difference is the kind of difference that five Justices of the Supreme Court referred to in the Jones case.

So we asked for a study, among other things, on these metadata issues because we think that the changing facts require some changing law, probably, but we do not say on the Constitution what our view is.

Senator COONS. Mr. Morell, if I might, the Review Group recommends replacing the Privacy and Civil Liberties Oversight Board with a new Civil Liberties Protection Board, and this new board would be empowered to review the privacy implications of all counterterrorism and foreign intelligence collections and have a new function to respond to whistleblowers and have new investigatory roles.

The current PCLOB is, I would suggest, absurdly underresourced relative to its scope of responsibility. The President's budget request includes only, I think it was, $3.1 million for the PCLOB. I may be wrong on that. Authorities without resources can be worse than no authorities at all because they provide a false sense of security.

I would be interested in your view of what budget would be sufficient to allow this new board to perform its mission.

Mr. MORELL. So I do not have a specific answer for you. That is not something we looked at. But it would be significantly more resources, in my view, than it currently receives today.

Senator COONS. Well, the intelligence community Inspector General, just to continue the examination, ostensibly exists within the IC to ensure legal compliance. It recently told us that it lacks the resources to conduct a thorough and full review of the 215 metadata program by the end of next year, so I think that reinforces the point that some significant increase in resources is needed to ensure the sort of oversight and accountability that I think all of us are working together to ensure.

Mr. Clarke, if I might, declassified FISC opinions have revealed that the NSA in the past exceeded Court-established bounds of the Section 215 bulk metadata collection program routinely and attempted to defend those actions in front of the Court. I think it is widely agreed now that this was a violation. Some of us would allege a serious one. My concern is that the NSA initially tried to defend its use of non-approved selectors, and I would be interested in your view about why the NSA attempted to defend its illegal actions as legal and what reforms are necessary to encourage the IC to come clean and admit its mistakes in cases like this.

Mr. CLARKE. Senator, I think there was a good-faith lack of understanding and lack of communication between NSA and the Court. I do not think there was any intentional attempt to circumvent the Court, but I think we had a bunch of engineers and computer scientists at NSA talking to a bunch of lawyers at the Court, and I think there was a lack of understanding about what each side was saying.

I believe as soon as the NSA learned of the Court's objections, they rectified the problem. So I think what this points to, these incidents point to, is the need for the Court to have more technical staff and resources. Just as the PCLOB, as you mentioned, is grossly underresourced, so is the Court.

Senator COONS. Are there any other elements of your recommendations that would deal with this cultural mismatch, at least as you have suggested you have got engineers and lawyers, anything about adding an advocate to—adding a more adversarial component to the deliberative process, would that also strengthen the Court's capabilities and oversight?

Mr. CLARKE. I think there are four or five recommendations that do that. One is a public advocate in the Court. Another is strengthening the technical ability of the Court staff. A third is creating, in the new civil liberties commission, a technology assessment staff.

Senator COONS. The review, if I might, Mr. Clarke—my last question—looks at two authorities, Section 702 and Section 215, and these are both sections about which there has been a lot of public debate and discussion. But the Review Group also recommends greater government disclosure about these and other surveillance authorities it possesses. But the report, appropriately and understandably, does not itself disclose any additional programs. What review, if any, did the group make of undisclosed programs? Or could you at least comment about whether lessons learned from such review is, in fact, reflected in the report?

Mr. CLARKE. Well, I think there is a great deal of metadata collected by the National Security Letter program, and we do speak to that in the recommendations. But there is also a great deal of communications-related information collected under Executive Order 12333. Public attention is focused on 215, but 215 produces a small percentage of the overall data that is collected.

Senator COONS. Thank you. Thank you to the whole panel for your testimony. I see I am past my time.

Senator BLUMENTHAL. Senator Klobuchar.

Senator KLOBUCHAR. Thank you, Mr. Chairman. I first want to note for the record that two of the witnesses were my law professors. Professor Stone taught evidence, and Professor Sunstein was my administrative law professor, and they both were fans of the Socratic method, so this is my revenge.

[Laughter.]

Senator KLOBUCHAR. Okay. So I first wanted to start with some of the recommendations here, and one of the most prominent recommendations of the Review Group was the U.S. Government should no longer hold the metadata, but data should be held by either the companies or a third party. I remember that General Alexander said he was open to this idea back in July, and I guess, starting with you, Mr. Clarke, do you think that this would lead to greater security, or do you think there could be more of a possibility of it being hacked? And then I guess I would ask the professors, do you think then the companies will be insisting on protections for liability?

Mr. CLARKE. Well, Senator, thankfully, I was not your professor. I note that there has been a very significant information compromise at NSA, well over a million documents stolen. So even NSA can have its information stolen. It is not just Target and other commercial entities.

Senator KLOBUCHAR. Thank you for bringing up my home town company.

Mr. CLARKE. Sorry about that.

Senator KLOBUCHAR. That is all right.

Mr. CLARKE. I am unaware of people's phone records going into the public record when they were stolen from phone companies. They are there now. We are not suggesting something new. The phone companies have the data. We are really suggesting that they keep it rather than the government.

If, rather than leave them at the phone companies, we went a third-party route, yes, you are absolutely right. The security of those records would have to be paramount, and I believe that security can be achieved from hackers. We spend a whole chapter in the report talking about how to do that. It is just that most people do not do it.

Senator KLOBUCHAR. Okay. How about the liability issue?

Mr. CLARKE. Liability, I think, is a matter of your providing safe harbor by legislation.

Senator KLOBUCHAR. Okay. One other recommendation was to create, which has, I know, been discussed before I got here, the public interest advocate at the Court to provide for a more adversarial process, to provide for someone to ensure that privacy and civil liberty interests were represented. Approximately what proportion of the cases should be substantively argued by a public interest advocate on privacy and liberty grounds? Do you see it as happening in every case or a percentage of the cases?

Mr. SUNSTEIN. Approximately small. The reason I say approximately small is that the overwhelming majority of the cases do not involve novel or difficult issues of law and policy. So, one thing we are focused on is the possibility that the public interest advocate would not have as many hours of engagement as a standard lawyer does just because a lot of the cases are routine.

We do not have an exact percentage, but where the issues of law or policy are novel, then there is a keen importance to making sure it is an adversary proceeding.

Senator KLOBUCHAR. Yes, I thought this was a good recommendation. Yesterday the Committee did receive a letter from Judge Bates, the Director of the Administrative Office of the U.S. Courts and a former presiding judge on FISC, in which he raised some significant questions about proposed reforms, including adding a standing special advocate to the Court, and recommended instead that the Court be allowed to appoint an advocate on a case-by-case basis. Does this make sense to you? I do not know if you want to——

Mr. SUNSTEIN. We admire Judge Bates and respect his views. We respectfully disagree with that one on the grounds that the judge sometimes is not in the ideal position to know whether a particular view needs representation, and that in our tradition standardly the judge does not decide whether one or another view gets a lawyer. And this is an unusual context, admittedly, but if there is a privacy or civil liberties concern, it is good to have someone who is specially authorized to take account of that concern in deciding whether to participate.

Senator KLOBUCHAR. That makes sense. The public revelation of the surveillance programs, particularly those targeting foreign leaders, has generated a strong outcry from some of our allies, including Germany and Brazil. And the Review Group recommended that the U.S. intelligence community limit surveillance focused on foreign leaders to instances where there is a clear need and that such intelligence requirements be subject to senior policymaker review.

I guess, first of all, I would ask—I think, Mr. Morell, would this be your area? In your view, did the surveillance of Prime Minister Merkel meet the standards that you are suggesting here?

Mr. MORELL. Ma'am, I cannot confirm or deny the surveillance of any particular foreign leader. I would say that I think it is absolutely important that policymakers make decisions about collection at that level, and that has not been the case heretofore.

Senator KLOBUCHAR. And the Review Group also recommended extending the protections of the Privacy Act of 1974 to foreign citizens. Is there a precedent for the U.S. Government or any other government to extend privacy protections to foreign citizens in its conduct of intelligence collection?

Mr. SWIRE. Thank you, Senator. On the Privacy Act, the Department of Homeland Security for several years has had a policy that we say should be adopted more broadly, which isl when there is a mixed system of records and there are U.S. and non-U.S. people in that, then the non-U.S. people would have access to those records as well. So we are building on the precedent from Homeland Security.

Senator KLOBUCHAR. Okay. Very good. Anyone want to add anything more?

[No response.]

Senator KLOBUCHAR. All right. Thank you.

Senator BLUMENTHAL. Thank you, Senator Klobuchar.

Senator Durbin.

Senator DURBIN. Thanks, Senator Blumenthal, and thank you all.

I regret that Osama bin Laden brings us to the airport about an hour earlier than we used to go, and I regret that Edward Snowden brings us together today. But I think we have to acknowledge the obvious. There is a public question now about privacy and whether the government is going too far. It is a question many of us contemplated in the past, but could never discuss openly. Now that this is a matter of public record, we have this hearing, as we should, to try to restore the confidence of the American people.

Several of you are authors, and I have read your works on a lot of different issues. But the issue before us today is one where the word is not even found in the Constitution—''privacy''—and what we can come to expect and what the Court might view as going too far, any court might view as going too far, and whether the court of public opinion would view as going too far.

When you consider the incredible advancement in telephone technology, smart mobile phones, the ubiquitous use of the Internet, is it time to revisit whether *Smith* v. *Maryland* is in line with the expectations of the American people about privacy? In a world that we live in where phone booths are viewed as some quaint anachronism and people stand up in the middle of a crowded place and broadcast their telephone conversations to everybody within earshot, where we know that commercial invasion of our personal privacy is taking place almost constantly, and the accumulation of information by our government is only a fraction of what the commercial sector is gathering about us every single day in every move we make, take a step back and get to altitude here and tell me what you think the issue of privacy looks like.

Mr. SUNSTEIN. Senator, from the 100,000-foot level, we do believe that in the current technological environment, if people use the Internet or the telephone or banks, it is right, certainly as a matter of public policy, to protect their privacy and to focus on striking the right balance between national security needs and the needs of government to get access to information that can protect us against those who would do us harm.

So we were not asked to investigate the Constitutional issue as if we were judges, but we were alert to your concerns, very much so, in offering our recommendations.

Senator DURBIN. And is it not a fact that if I could obtain anyone's phone logs of the actual phone numbers they called and know the names of the persons they called, I could probably draw some inference about them, their lives, maybe their intentions?

Mr. SUNSTEIN. Unquestionably. So metadata is not the same as content, but it is something that people are understandably skeptical of the idea that others get access to, especially the government, for exactly the reason you give.

Senator DURBIN. And if we let the telephone companies retain possession of this data and go after it as needed, what kind of obstacle does that create in going after bad guys, Boston bombers, where we might come up with a telephone number and need to know pretty quickly whether this is isolated or part of an international effort?

Mr. SUNSTEIN. If there is a need, either because something bad has happened in the recent past or because there are reasonable grounds to believe it is going to happen in the near or pretty near future, then if time is of the essence, there is no need to go to court. So we would design our recommendation and the legislation that would respond to the recommendation in a way that acknowledges that sometimes you have to move very fast.

Senator DURBIN. Senator Coons raised this question—I am sure it has been raised earlier before I came—about adding some balance to the FISA Court so that there is at least something akin to an adversarial proceeding or at least both sides of the issue are being heard. What do you feel, based on the work that you have done, is the most credible way to establish that?

Mr. SWIRE. Thank you, Senator. I will just say a couple things that are in our report.

One thing is that trying to think about who those people are institutionally is something that I think deserves some public attention. The people who would be advocates would have to have a clearance because they would have to be working in the FISA Court. You would want them to have some continuity over time so that the last case is known to them enough so that the next case makes sense. And it might not be a full-time job because it is only occasionally that the big minimization cases happen.

Senator DURBIN. Who would they work for?

Mr. SWIRE. Well, and so we suggest some ideas that have not been as much discussed in the public before that. One idea would be to put it at the PCLOB, the Privacy Board or whatever you call it going forward, because they have a lot of other jobs to do and they have lawyers. Another possibility is to put it out for bid so that some law firm or public interest group would have three or five years where they are doing it. They have a day job, but when it is important to do it, they are there to do it.

The concern is if you just sort of pop in and out, you would not have the technological and other context to do it well, and if you sit there full time, you have nothing to do for weeks at a time, possibly.

Senator DURBIN. We have this quaint concept of an Inspector General in departments, working at the department but not for the department, literally charged with taking a look from an outside point of view, and most of them emerge with some credibility because of this relationship. Is that something that we could build on?

Mr. SWIRE. Historically, my understanding is the IGs have not had a legal function, that putting a legal office in the IG would be—you are saying it—but my understanding is that they have had fraud, waste, and abuse but not being the best lawyers you can get. If you want the best lawyers you can get for privacy and civil liberties arguing with the Court and with the very great lawyers in the Department of Justice, thinking about how to staff that so you will have really good people available, and they probably need something else to do the days of the week when they are not doing this because it is not that many cases.

Senator DURBIN. I might just close by saying two things.

First, the pending appropriations bill, the omnibus bill, contains some provisions which I have added that will finally make public, as much as can be made public, a lot of specific data about what has been collected, why it has been collected, and what the result of the collections has been. It has been an issue that has been important to me for a long time, and it is going to be part of the bipartisan bill.

And, finally, I support what Senator Blumenthal is trying to do to make sure these FISA Courts are more balanced in the appointees. Not to take anything away from the current process, but I think if there were more diversity in the selection, there would be more confidence in the outcome. I think his legislation is a good move.

Thank you.

Senator BLUMENTHAL. Thank you, Senator Durbin.

Just to pursue Senator Durbin's point about how to house the special advocate or constitutional advocate or public advocate, I think the key question that he asked is: Who does she or he work for? Who is the client? And my concept in advancing it originally was always that the client is the individual or group whose constitutional rights may be imperiled. In other words, it really is the Constitution. And the appearance, again, we talked earlier about appearance and perception being important. Housing is important from a perception standpoint. If the public defenders in federal courts—and I dealt with a lot of them as a U.S. Attorney—were housed in the prosecutor's office, clients coming to be defended would have a totally different perception, even though it might actually save money to put them in the prosecutor's office.

So I think there is a very important analogy here, and that in the federal system we have federal public defenders who are full-time, they are not ad hoc, although for a long time people were represented by—and still are in State courts—people sort of hauled into the process to do their duty with minimal pay while juggling other duties, and sometimes not clear that they had the experience to handle a particular case. And that is why I have advocated a full-time, institutionalized, separate office that is independent, as independent as possible, because perception is so important. And I want to thank you all for giving thought to the excellent kind of questions that Senator Durbin and Senator Coons and Senator Klobuchar have raised.

One last point, again, to pursue Senator Durbin's question. *Smith* v. *Maryland* is about as outdated as I think any Supreme Court could possibly be, given that it was dealing with a different system of information gathering at a different time, not only with payphones but literally the wires, the mechanism, the infrastructure was so different. And I think the elephant in the room here is really the Supreme Court. Many of our colleagues have said, well, we ought to wait for the Supreme Court. But we all know that the Supreme Court is not necessarily an absolutely clear and non-controversial source of law. And we have an equal responsibility, the Congress under the United States Constitution has an equal responsibility to protect the Constitution, indeed to define the Constitution. And that is why your work, I think, has been very, very important, because you have really, as I mentioned earlier, not only given us some guidance but also great credibility to the direction that I believe and hope the President will go.

So if there are other comments, we are going to hold this record open for one week. Senator Sessions has asked me to place in the record a *Wall Street Journal* opinion article by former Attorney General Mukasey. It is entitled, ''The Era of Unreality in NSA Reform.''

[The article appears as a submission for the record.]

Senator BLUMENTHAL. And we will hold this record open for a week, and thank you all, gentlemen.

[Whereupon, at 4:55 p.m., the Committee was adjourned.]

APPENDIX

ADDITIONAL MATERIAL SUBMITTED FOR THE RECORD

Witness List

Hearing before the
Senate Committee on the Judiciary

On

"Hearing on the Report of the President's Review Group on Intelligence and Communications Technologies"

Tuesday, January 14, 2014
Dirksen Senate Office Building, Room 226
2:30 p.m.

The Honorable Richard A. Clarke

The Honorable Michael Morell

Professor Geoffrey Stone

The Honorable Cass Sunstein

Professor Peter Swire

Statement of Senator Patrick Leahy (D-Vt.),
Chairman, Senate Judiciary Committee,
Hearing on the Report of the President's Review Group
on Intelligence and Communications Technologies
January 14, 2014

Today, we will hear from the President's Review Group on Intelligence and Communications Technologies. This is the first time they have appeared together publicly since their ground-breaking report was released last month.

The Review Group's report addresses some of the weightiest issues that we will confront in the coming years. Technology will continue to advance in ways we cannot even imagine. More and more data will be created by all of us as each day passes. When should our government be allowed to collect and use that data? To what extent does the massive collection of data improve our national security? And what will the answers to these questions mean for privacy and free expression in the 21st century?

All three branches of government are grappling with whether to allow the NSA's dragnet collection of Americans' domestic phone records to continue, and we are finally doing so with full public participation in that debate. The Review Group makes an important contribution to this conversation. While we must always consider ongoing threats to national security, the report urges policymakers to consider all of the risks associated with this and other intelligence activities: the risk to individual privacy, to free expression and freedom of association, to an open and decentralized Internet, to America's relationships with other nations, to trade and commerce, and to maintaining the public trust.

The most critical factor in deciding whether to conduct any particular intelligence activity is an assessment of its value. This is particularly important in evaluating the phone records program conducted under Section 215 of the USA PATRIOT Act. As I have said repeatedly, I have concluded that this phone records program is not uniquely valuable enough to justify the massive intrusion on Americans' privacy.

The Review Group likewise concluded that the program has not been essential, saying: "The information contributed to terrorist investigations by the use of section 215 telephony meta-data was not essential to preventing attacks and could readily have been obtained in a timely manner using conventional section 215 orders." And a few pages later: "Section 215 has generated relevant information in only a small number of cases, and there has been no instance in which NSA could say with confidence that the outcome would have been different without the section 215 telephony meta-data program."

In addition to the concerns about the utility of this program, I also question its constitutionality. Although the Review Group report is careful not to make a legal judgment about the program, it acknowledges the ramifications of the extraordinarily broad legal theory on which the program is based. The report explains that nothing in Section 215, as interpreted by the FISA Court, would preclude the mass collection of Americans' personal information beyond phone records. In addition, one member of the Review Group has publicly concluded that the program as currently constituted violates the Fourth Amendment.

The privacy implications of this sort of massive surveillance in the digital age cannot be overstated, and the Review Group's report provides some valuable insights. Some argue that there is nothing wrong with the NSA's program because it is "just collecting metadata." But the report reminds us that keeping a record of every phone call an individual has made over the course of several years "can reveal an enormous amount about that individual's private life." It further explains that in the 21st century, revealing private information to third party services "does not reflect a lack of concern for the privacy of the information, but a necessary accommodation to the realities of modern life." The report appropriately questions whether we can continue to draw a rational line between metadata and content. This is a critically important question given that many of our surveillance laws depend upon the distinction between the two.

These insights are also important as we take up reforms to the National Security Letter statutes. Using NSLs, the FBI can obtain detailed information about individuals' communications records, financial transactions, and credit reports without judicial approval. Recipients of NSLs are subject to permanent gag orders. Senator Durbin and I have been fighting to impose additional safeguards on this controversial authority for years – to limit their use, to ensure that NSL gag orders comply with the First Amendment, and to provide recipients of NSLs with a meaningful opportunity for judicial review. The Review Group report makes a series of important recommendations to change the way National Security Letters operate. These recommendations have not generated the same attention that other issues have, but they should.

The report also recommends creating an institutional Public Interest Advocate at the FISA Court, a proposal that I strongly support. I am concerned that merely allowing for an amicus to participate at the FISA Court from time to time will neither improve the substantive outcome of the proceedings, nor rebuild public confidence in the process.

I suspect none of us on this Committee agrees with all of the report's recommendations, but we are privileged to hear directly from this distinguished panel today. They have written a thoughtful report worthy of careful consideration, and I applaud the members of the Review Group for their public service.

The stakes are high. This is a debate about Americans' fundamental relationship with their government – about whether the government should have the power to create massive databases of information about its citizens. I believe strongly that we must impose stronger limits on government surveillance powers – and I am confident that most Vermonters, and most Americans, agree with me. We need to get this right.

# # # # #

PREPARED STATEMENT OF HON. DIANNE FEINSTEIN

Opening Statement of Senator Feinstein
Judiciary Committee Hearing on President's Review Group on Intelligence and Communications Technologies
Tuesday, January 14, 2014

Thank you, Chairman Leahy.

I'd like to welcome the panel and appreciate their being here today. For the information of other Members, the Intelligence Committee met with three of the Review Groups members in a hearing last week – Mr. Sunstein, Mr. Swire, and Mr. Stone. It's good to see you again, along with Michael Morell and Richard Clarke.

I noted then, and want to re-iterate now, that there are a number of constructive recommendations in their report, in particular with respect to the need to improve the security clearance process, better protect information in the government's hands, and strengthen whistleblower protections for Intelligence Community employees.

Many of these provisions, as well as measures providing for additional transparency into intelligence collection programs where possible, are included in the FISA improvements legislation and the Fiscal Year 2014 intelligence authorization bill reported favorably by the Senate Intelligence Committee last fall with strong bipartisan votes. (The FISA Improvements bill passed 11-4 and FY 14 Intelligence Authorization bill passed 13-2.)

However, I am concerned by a number of other findings and recommendations in the report, and want to repeat briefly some of my concerns and some of what we discussed last week.

First and foremost is the recommendation to replace the current NSA call records program operated under the Business Records provision of FISA with one where the phone companies or a private third party hold the records and the government must go to the FISA Court each time it seeks to query this data.

The Intelligence Committee looked at this approach in our deliberations concerning the NSA program both before and after the program was leaked to the media and found that it likely would increase significantly the cost of the program to taxpayers (at least in the short-term); require new statutes be passed to, among other things, compel private parties to store the metadata and new network infrastructures to be developed for the government to receive and process the data; cause a delay of up to several days in the government's ability to obtain information in response to a query; and do precious little to enhance privacy protections, as the data would still be stored, but by one or more private entities that are not subject to the same oversight and accountability requirements as NSA.

Moreover, it should say something that this alternative approach is strongly opposed not only by the telecommunications providers but also by privacy groups who oppose requiring the telecom companies to hold and search this data.

The Review Group acknowledges in their report that there has been no finding of any "official efforts to suppress dissent or any intent to intrude into people's private lives without legal justification." Last week, members of the Review Group testified to the Senate Intelligence Committee that their report has been misunderstood by the media and that they believe the NSA program has value and should be maintained, albeit in a different form.

Significantly, in an op-ed published in the *Washington Post* on December 27th, one member of the Review Group, Mr. Morell, wrote to "correct the record" and stated that the NSA program "would likely have prevented 9/11. And it has the potential to prevent the next 9/11." In fact, Mr. Morell calls for an expansion of the program.

When I raised this op-ed with the three Review Group witnesses, they agreed with Mr. Morell's comments, and I hope to ask all the panelists today to say for the record whether they believe the 215 program may have been able to alert the government to the 9/11 plot, and that it could prove instrumental in thwarting a future attack.

Let me note here two other areas that we discussed last week.

First is the Review Group's recommendation number 15, which matches a section in the SSCI FISA Improvements Act. We both believe that the NSA should have additional, limited statutory authority to continue surveillance when a known counterterrorism target outside the United States travels to the United States. Under current law, NSA must stop surveillance that has been lawfully conducted, either under Section 702 of FISA or under Executive Order 12333, until the government can go to the Court for an individual warrant under Title I of FISA. That process can take days, and occurs precisely when the individual may be in position to carry out an attack.

Secondly, the Review Group's recommendations 7 through 10 address public transparency with respect to the government's use of national security letters, FISA orders, and similar tools used in national security investigations. Recommendation 9 in particular states that companies who receive national security letters or FISA orders and produce information as a result should be allowed to periodically disclose to the public information on the numbers of requests and related general information. A number of technology companies, including Apple, Facebook, Google, LinkedIn, Microsoft, Twitter, Yahoo, and others, have sought this authority – not to disclose specifics of whose account information is being sought any why, but to provide general statistics so they can publicly describe and defend their cooperation with the government.

The companies have noted that they are losing business to foreign competitors because of suspicions about the extent of their cooperation with the government. I know Sen. Franken has introduced legislation to provide companies with the authority they seek and I'd like to work with Sen. Franken to increase transparency in this area because I believe it is possible to do so in a way that still protects national security.

Thank you, Mr. Chairman, for the opportunity to make these opening remarks.

QUESTIONS

Senator Grassley's Questions for the Record from

Senate Committee on the Judiciary

"Hearing on the Report of the President's Review Group on Intelligence and Communications
Technologies"

January 14, 2014

Questions for the President's Review Group on Intelligence and Communications Technologies

1. Application of the Privacy Act to Non-United States Persons

The Review Group's report recommends that the intelligence community apply the Privacy Act of 1974
to non-U.S. persons. This is currently the policy of the Department of Homeland Security (DHS).
However, a former Director of the National Counterterrorism Center wrote that he "spent literally years
negotiating for access and retention to certain DHS data about non-U.S. persons and often the Privacy Act
protections posed significant practical obstacles." He further wrote that this recommendation "should be
read with extreme skepticism as it would likely do far more harm than good."

    a.   Why would extending such a policy across the intelligence community would do more
good than harm? Specifically, what are the benefits of such a policy for the United
States?

    b.   What effect would implementation of this recommendation have on information sharing
about suspected foreign terrorists within the U.S. government? What is the basis for this
conclusion?

2. Recommended Changes to the Section 215 Bulk Metadata Program

The Review Group's report recommended that metadata collected pursuant to the Section 215 program no
longer be held by the NSA, but rather be stored with the communications providers or a third party, and
that the government be required to obtain an order from the FISC before querying the metadata.

    a.   What effect would implementation of the recommendation that NSA no longer hold the
metadata have on the FBI's ability to use the metadata, especially in cases when speed is
important? What is the basis for this conclusion? Do you know, for example, whether
third parties maintain the data in the same format, or have the same searching capabilities
as the government?

    b.   Please describe in detail the basis for the conclusion in the report that creative
engineering approaches could help provide the government with similar functionality to
search the metadata if it were to be held by a third party.

    c.   How much would implementing this recommendation cost the government if it were to
pay for third parties to hold the metadata? What is the basis for this conclusion?

    d.   What is your assessment of the privacy risks if third parties were to hold the metadata?
What is the basis for this conclusion?

    e.   What do you believe is a reasonable period of time for the government to transition to
and implement a system in which third parties hold the metadata?

f.   What effect would implementation of the recommendation that the government obtain a court order have on the FBI's ability to use the metadata, especially in cases when speed is important? What is the basis for this conclusion?

g.   In developing this recommendation, did you consider the government's experience during the period when the FISC required it to obtain court approval for queries of the metadata? What was that experience? For example, did you consider the length of time that it took for court approval during that period, how that increased time affected investigations, and whether that process led the government to forgo queries that it might otherwise have made if it had not needed a court order?

3. Metadata (for Director Morell only)

Director Morell, you testified that that there is "quite a bit of content in metadata" and that there is not "a sharp distinction between metadata and content."

a.   For clarification, under the Section 215 telephony metadata program, as your report stated, metadata "does not include the content of calls," correct? In other words, the information that is collected under this program includes only the telephone numbers that originate and receive the calls, and the date and time of the calls. It does not include, for example, the identity of the subscriber or caller, or any of the words they may have spoken during the conversation.

b.   Director Morell, does your testimony on this point presuppose the government querying the metadata and then marrying it with other information? If so, isn't the government only permitted to take these steps when it has a reasonable and articulable suspicion that a phone number is connected to terrorism? Can the government learn anything about a specific individual's private life merely by collecting this metadata, if it is never queried or combined with other information?

4. National Security Letters

The Review Group's report recommended that National Security Letters ("NSLs") should only be issued upon a judicial finding, and only when there are "reasonable grounds to believe that the particular information sought is relevant to an authorized investigation intended to protect against international terrorism or clandestine intelligence activities."

However, according to the comments of the Judiciary transmitted to the Committee by Judge Bates through his letter of January 10, 2014, this recommendation could "increase the FISC's annual caseload severalfold." He further stated that "the sheer volume of new cases…would transform the FISC from an institution that is primarily focused on a relatively small number of cases that involve the most intrusive or expansive forms of intelligence collection to one primarily engaged in processing a much larger number of more routine, subpoena-type cases."

The FBI issues more than 20,000 NSLs each year for data such as telephone subscriber information, as well as banking and credit-card records. The data does not include phone call content. FBI Director James Comey said that NSLs are "a very important tool" that is "essential" to the work of the FBI. He also stated that adopting this recommendation would "actually make it harder for us to do national security investigations than bank fraud investigations."

a.   What benefit will be achieved by requiring the FISC to review all NSLs, given the relatively low relevance standard that the group recommends?

b.   What effect would implementation of this recommendation have on both the operation of the FISC and the FBI's ability to investigate national security cases? What is the basis for this conclusion?

c.   What effect would implementation of this recommendation have on the FISC's budget and additional judges required? What is the basis for this conclusion?

d.   Why does it make sense for the FISC to pre-approve NSLs when courts do not pre-approve grand jury subpoenas? In either case, if a criminal prosecution results, doesn't a defendant have the opportunity to challenge the use of these investigative tools if they are used unlawfully or improperly?

5. Special Advocate

In your report, you recommended that an institutional privacy advocate should be appointed to represent the public's interest before the FISC. As set forth in this recommendation, the advocate could intervene in any case without permission from the presiding judge. However, the comments of the Judiciary transmitted to the Committee by Judge Bates warned against such an approach, for a variety of reasons.

a.   What effect would implementation of this recommendation have on the FISC's budget and additional judges required? What is the basis for this conclusion?

b.   What effect would implementation of this recommendation have on both the operation of the FISC and the FBI's ability to investigate national security cases? What is the basis for this conclusion?

c.   Do you agree with the comments from the Judiciary that in the vast majority of matters before the FISC, involving an advocate in the process would be both unnecessary and counterproductive? Why or why not?

d.   Do you agree with the comments from the Judiciary that in the vast majority of matters before the FISC, involving an advocate in the process would result in more protections for suspected foreign terrorists than U.S. citizens? Why or why not? Do you believe this is desirable? Why or why not?

e.   Do you believe that FISC judges are capable of accurately assessing whether a matter requires the involvement of the special advocate? What is the basis for this conclusion?

f.   Do you agree with the comments from the Judiciary that involving an advocate in the process could actually result in the court receiving less information on which to make a decision, because the government might be reluctant to share sensitive information with an institutional advocate and would no longer be bound by the heightened duties associated with *ex parte* practice? Why or why not?

6.   For each of the above-mentioned recommendations, as well as all others listed in the report, please list the stakeholders or interested parties with which you discussed the recommendation, very briefly summarize the feedback the stakeholders or interested parties provided, and indicate whether the stakeholder or interested party (a) agreed with the recommendation or urged its adoption, and why; or (b) disagreed with the recommendation or urged that it not be adopted, and why.

RESPONSES OF THE PRESIDENT'S REVIEW GROUP MEMBERS TO QUESTIONS SUBMITTED BY SENATOR CHUCK GRASSLEY

Senator Grassley's Questions for the Record from

Senate Committee on the Judiciary

"Hearing on the Report of the President's Review Group on Intelligence and Communications Technologies"

January 14, 2014

Questions for the President's Review Group on Intelligence and Communications Technologies

1. Application of the Privacy Act to Non-United States Persons

The Review Group's report recommends that the intelligence community apply the Privacy Act of 1974 to non-U.S. persons. This is currently the policy of the Department of Homeland Security (DHS). However, a former Director of the National Counterterrorism Center wrote that he "spent literally years negotiating for access and retention to certain DHS data about non-U.S. persons and often the Privacy Act protections posed significant practical obstacles." He further wrote that this recommendation "should be read with extreme skepticism as it would likely do far more harm than good."

    a.   Why would extending such a policy across the intelligence community would do more good than harm? Specifically, what are the benefits of such a policy for the United States?

    b.   What effect would implementation of this recommendation have on information sharing about suspected foreign terrorists within the U.S. government? What is the basis for this conclusion?

Our recommendation would apply the Privacy Act of 1974 to non-U.S. persons in the same limited way as the Department of Homeland Security has done for several years. Notably, the Privacy Act would apply to "mixed" systems of records, which are systems of records where U.S. persons already have access and correction rights under the Privacy Act. For these "mixed" systems, the agency already must have in place an established procedure for responding to the limited number of access and correction requests that are made in practice. The additional administrative burden of responding in the same fashion to requests from both U.S. and non-U.S. persons, based on our interviews with those who have administered these systems, would be small.

The differential treatment of U.S. persons and non-U.S. persons under the Privacy Act has been a recurring source of concern from allies, notably including member states of the European Union, which has made a right to access a principal issue in data privacy negotiations to date. These negotiations, in turn, have been closely linked in statements by E.U. officials to negotiations for the free-trade agreement known as the Trans-Atlantic Trade and Partnership. By providing the same access rights both to citizens and non-citizens, as is the practice in the E.U., the recommendation addresses an important ongoing issue in negotiations with our leading trading partners in

Europe. Addressing this issue is consistent with the Presidential Policy Directive 28, which takes steps to treat non-U.S. persons similarly to U.S. persons where feasible.

Based on our briefings from multiple agencies, we believe the recommendation would not have a major impact on information sharing about suspected foreign terrorists. As noted in our report, the Privacy Act's requirements do not apply to classified computer systems or to law-enforcement sensitive/investigative information. We were informed that the FBI already applies the Privacy Act in the same manner for national security investigations as it does for other records covered by the Act. In addition, our recommendation creates an exception provision, so that it would not apply where an agency "provides specific and persuasive reasons not to do so."

2. Recommended Changes to the Section 215 Bulk Metadata Program

The Review Group's report recommended that metadata collected pursuant to the Section 215 program no longer be held by the NSA, but rather be stored with the communications providers or a third party, and that the government be required to obtain an order from the FISC before querying the metadata.

a. What effect would implementation of the recommendation that NSA no longer hold the metadata have on the FBI's ability to use the metadata, especially in cases when speed is important? What is the basis for this conclusion? Do you know, for example, whether third parties maintain the data in the same format, or have the same searching capabilities as the government?

When we met with the NSA, we were informed that it was not uncomfortable with this alternative and that its principal concern was the reluctance of the service providers to bear this responsibility. As we note in the Report, there will be transitional issues in moving from the existing system to one or another of the alternatives, and those issues deserve careful attention, but we believe that they can be managed and that the resulting program will operate efficiently. Our Report discusses relevant concerns and notes an alternative.

b. Please describe in detail the basis for the conclusion in the report that creative engineering approaches could help provide the government with similar functionality to search the metadata if it were to be held by a third party.

See our response to 2a. Given the extraordinary technological capacities of the NSA, we believe that problem can be managed if the NSA is asked to do so.

c. How much would implementing this recommendation cost the government if it were to pay for third parties to hold the metadata? What is the basis for this conclusion?

As we note in the Report, we recognize that there are costs involved. In the grand scheme of things, however, these costs seem reasonable and justified, relative to the alternative. The protection of individual privacy and the promotion of public trust are important goals.

d. What is your assessment of the privacy risks if third parties were to hold the metadata? What is the basis for this conclusion?

There are always privacy risks, regardless of who holds the metadata. Laws and processes should be in place to minimize those risks. The special risk in this context, however, is the risk that the government itself might misuse the data. Because government is so powerful, and is thus uniquely capable of doing great harm, that risk is at the very core of our constitutional protection of privacy. As our history teaches, the special concern in this context is that in the future, misguided government officials might use this data for illegitimate political ends. That particular risk – which threatens the integrity of our democracy – is much greater when the data is held by the government than when it is left in private hands.

e. What do you believe is a reasonable period of time for the government to transition to and implement a system in which third parties hold the metadata?

We did not offer an opinion on that question. In our judgment, the transition should take place as expeditiously as reasonably possible.

f. What effect would implementation of the recommendation that the government obtain a court order have on the FBI's ability to use the metadata, especially in cases when speed is important? What is the basis for this conclusion?

Consistent with standard practice, we recommend an exception to the requirement of a court order whenever speed is of the essence and the need to obtain a court order would seriously impair the FBI's ability to fulfill its responsibilities. We therefore think this should have no effect

on the FBI's ability to use the metadata in an appropriate manner.

g. In developing this recommendation, did you consider the government's experience during the period when the FISC required it to obtain court approval for queries of the metadata? What was that experience? For example, did you consider the length of time that it took for court approval during that period, how that increased time affected investigations, and whether that process led the government to forgo queries that it might otherwise have made if it had not needed a court order?

We recognize that, during this unusual period, the process was slow. This was no doubt due to the fact that the FISC was unaccustomed to dealing with such orders. We are hopeful that this would not be a problem once the process is regularized. After all, the FISC deals regularly with requests for court orders for other types of foreign intelligence surveillance, including order under section 215, and ordinary courts deal every day with search warrant requests in an expeditious and efficient manner. There is no reason why the FISC cannot do the same.

3. Metadata (for Director Morell only)

Director Morell, you testified that that there is "quite a bit of content in metadata" and that there is not "a sharp distinction between metadata and content."

a. For clarification, under the Section 215 telephony metadata program, as your report stated, metadata "does not include the content of calls," correct? In other words, the information that is collected under this program includes only the telephone numbers that originate and receive the calls, and the date and time of the calls. It does not include, for example, the identity of the subscriber or caller, or any of the words they may have spoken during the conversation.

b. Director Morell, does your testimony on this point presuppose the government querying the metadata and then marrying it with other information? If so, isn't the government only permitted to take these steps when it has a reasonable and articulable suspicion that a phone number is connected to terrorism? Can the government learn anything about a specific individual's private life merely by collecting this metadata, if it is never queried or combined with other information?

3. Question Regarding Metadata and Content (per the Committee's request, this question was answered specifically by Mr. Morell):

Senator Grassley is correct in noting that the telephony metadata held by NSA under Section 215 of the Patriot Act – by itself – does not contain content. The

Senator is also correct in noting that for that metadata to reveal content, it would have to be married with other data.

The point I (Mr. Morell) was trying to make is that it is possible to go from the seemingly innocuous metadata under 215 to highly personal information with very little effort, thus creating a potential risk to privacy and civil liberties. For example, an individual, acting inappropriately, bringing together metadata under 215 and only the internet, could easily reveal the identity of the caller and the identities of individuals and entities that he/she called – and with that information learn a great deal about the caller, his/her life, and lifestyle.

4. National Security Letters

The Review Group's report recommended that National Security Letters ("NSLs") should only be issued upon a judicial finding, and only when there are "reasonable grounds to believe that the particular information sought is relevant to an authorized investigation intended to protect against international terrorism or clandestine intelligence activities."

However, according to the comments of the Judiciary transmitted to the Committee by Judge Bates through his letter of January 10, 2014, this recommendation could "increase the FISC's annual caseload severalfold." He further stated that "the sheer volume of new cases…would transform the FISC from an institution that is primarily focused on a relatively small number of cases that involve the most intrusive or expansive forms of intelligence collection to one primarily engaged in processing a much larger number of more routine, subpoena-type cases."

The FBI issues more than 20,000 NSLs each year for data such as telephone subscriber information, as well as banking and credit-card records. The data does not include phone call content. FBI Director James Comey said that NSLs are "a very important tool" that is "essential" to the work of the FBI. He also stated that adopting this recommendation would "actually make it harder for us to do national security investigations than bank fraud investigations."

a.   What benefit will be achieved by requiring the FISC to review all NSLs, given the relatively low relevance standard that the group recommends?

As the Supreme Court has long recognized, the requirement of a court order is essential to mitigate the inherent risks of allowing persons engaged in the "competitive enterprise of ferreting out crime" to decide for themselves when a search is appropriate. That is, quite simply, why the Constitution ordinarily requires search warrants. In the absence of a persuasive reason not to require a judicial order, judicial involvement should presumptively be the preferred process. This is why section 215 requires court orders when the government seeks to obtain information from third parties in circumstances quite similar to those for which NSLs are used. Moreover, experience shows that there have been significant problems in the past with the use of NSLs, problems that demonstrate the need for judicial oversight.

b.   What effect would implementation of this recommendation have on both the operation of the FISC and the FBI's ability to investigate national security cases? What is the basis for this conclusion?

As we note in the Report, this recommendation would add substantial new responsibilities to the work of the FISC. Additional judges – or magistrate judges – would be needed. Beyond that, we do not see any reason why giving this responsibility to the FISC – a responsibility it already has in the implementation of section 215 – would be in any way unreasonable.

c.   What effect would implementation of this recommendation have on the FISC's budget and additional judges required? What is the basis for this conclusion?

See the response to question 4b.

d.   Why does it make sense for the FISC to pre-approve NSLs when courts do not pre-approve grand jury subpoenas? In either case, if a criminal prosecution results, doesn't a defendant have the opportunity to challenge the use of these investigative tools if they are used unlawfully or improperly?

Grand jury subpoenas are typically designed to enable criminal prosecutions. When such prosecutions take place, there is an opportunity for judicial review of the legality of any subpoenas. In addition, the grand jury subpoena process is not classified. There is thus considerable opportunity for public oversight. NSL are classified. Criminal prosecutions in which the details of NSLs are revealed are extremely rare. For the most part, it is a secret process. This is, for the most part, appropriate. But it is why there is a greater need for independent judicial review of the process. Section 215 provides the more appropriate analogy than grand jury subpoenas, and Congress wisely recognized in section 215 the need for judicial orders.

5. Special Advocate

In your report, you recommended that an institutional privacy advocate should be appointed to represent the public's interest before the FISC. As set forth in this recommendation, the advocate could intervene in any case without permission from the presiding judge. However, the comments of the Judiciary transmitted to the Committee by Judge Bates warned against such an approach, for a variety of reasons.

h.   What effect would implementation of this recommendation have on the FISC's budget and additional judges required? What is the basis for this conclusion? – As noted in our transmittal letter, we did not explore the budgetary and related questions raised by our various recommendations, and offered those recommendations subject to budgetary constraints.

i.   What effect would implementation of this recommendation have on both the operation of the FISC and the FBI's ability to investigate national security cases? What is the basis for this conclusion?

We believe that the recommendation would have no adverse effects. Our recommendation is designed only for cases raising serious questions of law, and in such cases, an adversary process is typically an important safeguard.

j. Do you agree with the comments from the Judiciary that in the vast majority of matters before the FISC, involving an advocate in the process would be both unnecessary and counterproductive? Why or why not?

We do not disagree with this statement (though the word "vast" might be a bit too strong). In the majority of cases, the relevant issues are relatively routine, and a public advocate would not be necessary.

k. Do you agree with the comments from the Judiciary that in the vast majority of matters before the FISC, involving an advocate in the process would result in more protections for suspected foreign terrorists than U.S. citizens? Why or why not? Do you believe this is desirable? Why or why not?

We agree that in most matters, an advocate would not be necessary or desirable. We do believe that for serious questions of law or policy, involving an advocate would not result in "more protections" for suspected foreign terrorists than for Americans. An adversary process would, in such cases, fit with our traditions.

l. Do you believe that FISC judges are capable of accurately assessing whether a matter requires the involvement of the special advocate? What is the basis for this conclusion?

We would not question the ability of the FISC judges in any way, but we believe that in our system, judges should not decide whether important interests or values should receive representation. That is the job of people whose interests or values are at stake. For this reason, we would not give the judges the power to decide that question.

m. Do you agree with the comments from the Judiciary that involving an advocate in the process could actually result in the court receiving less information on which to make a decision, because the government might be reluctant to share sensitive information with an institutional advocate and would no longer be bound by the heightened duties associated with *ex parte* practice? Why or why not?

There might be a risk of such an unintended outcome, for the reasons outlined in those comments, but when serious legal questions are involved, we believe that the risk is outweighed by the value of having an adversary proceeding.

6.   For each of the above-mentioned recommendations, as well as all others listed in the report, please list the stakeholders or interested parties with which you discussed the recommendation, very briefly summarize the feedback the stakeholders or interested parties provided, and indicate whether the stakeholder or interested party (a) agreed with the recommendation or urged its adoption, and why; or (b) disagreed with the recommendation or urged that it not be adopted, and why.

The Review Group no longer exists, and hence we no longer have an available staff, but the full list of the people with whom we met can be found in our report. The public comments we received are also publicly available, and the oral comments we received in our various meetings were consistent with the written comments that are publicly available.

MISCELLANEOUS SUBMISSIONS FOR THE RECORD

ADMINISTRATIVE OFFICE OF THE
UNITED STATES COURTS

HONORABLE JOHN D. BATES
Director

WASHINGTON, D.C. 20544

January 13, 2014

Honorable Charles E. Grassley
Ranking Member
Committee on the Judiciary
United States Senate
Washington, DC 20510

Dear Senator Grassley:

To better address the continuing interest from several Congressional committees in the views of the Judiciary regarding potential changes to foreign intelligence surveillance law and practice, I am writing to provide the following perspectives on certain proposals currently under consideration.

Traditionally, the views of the Judiciary on legislative matters are expressed through the Judicial Conference of the United States, for which I serve as Secretary. However, because the matters at issue here relate to special expertise and experience of only a small number of judges on two specialized courts, the Conference has not at this time been engaged to deliberate on them. In my capacity as Director of the Administrative Office of the United States Courts, I have responsibility for facilitating the administration of the federal courts and, furthermore, the Chief Justice of the United States has requested that I act as a liaison for the Judiciary on matters concerning the Foreign Intelligence Surveillance Act (FISA). In considering such matters, I benefit from having served as Presiding Judge of the Foreign Intelligence Surveillance Court (FISC).

Enclosed is a document setting forth the Judiciary's comments concerning certain potential changes to FISA and proceedings before the FISC and the Foreign Intelligence Surveillance Court of Review. In preparing this document, I have consulted with the current Presiding Judges of the FISC and the Court of Review, as well as with other judges who serve or have served on those courts. For the sake of convenience, throughout the enclosed document (and in the summary below) I use the terms "we" and "our" to describe the Judiciary's institutional perspectives.

A TRADITION OF SERVICE TO THE FEDERAL JUDICIARY

Our comments focus on the operational impact on the Courts from certain proposed changes, but we do not express views on the policy choices that the political branches are considering. We are hopeful, of course, that any changes will both enhance our national security and provide appropriate respect and protection for privacy and civil-liberties interests. Achieving that goal undoubtedly will require great attention to the details of any adjustments that are undertaken. For example, it may not be important whether an outside participant in certain matters before the Courts is labeled an *amicus curiae* or public advocate; what matters is the specific structure and role of such a participant.

The following is a summary of our key comments:

- It is imperative that any significant increase in workload for the Courts be accompanied by a commensurate increase in resources.

- Some proposed changes would profoundly increase the Courts' workload. Even if additional financial, personnel, and physical resources were provided, any substantial increase in workload could nonetheless prove disruptive to the Courts' ability to perform their duties, including responsibilities under FISA and the Constitution to ensure that the privacy interests of United States citizens and others are adequately protected.

- The participation of a privacy advocate is unnecessary—and could prove counterproductive—in the vast majority of FISA matters, which involve the application of a probable cause or other factual standard to case-specific facts and typically implicate the privacy interests of few persons other than the specified target. Given the nature of FISA proceedings, the participation of an advocate would neither create a truly adversarial process nor constructively assist the Courts in assessing the facts, as the advocate would be unable to communicate with the target or conduct an independent investigation. Advocate involvement in run-of-the-mill FISA matters would substantially hamper the work of the Courts without providing any countervailing benefit in terms of privacy protection or otherwise; indeed, such pervasive participation could actually undermine the Courts' ability to receive complete and accurate information on the matters before them.

- In those matters in which an outside voice could be helpful, it is critical that the participation of an advocate be structured in a manner that maximizes assistance to the Courts and minimizes disruption to their work. An advocate appointed at the discretion of the Courts is likely to be helpful, whereas a standing advocate with independent authority to intervene at will could actually be counterproductive.

- Drastically expanding the FISC's caseload by assigning to it in excess of 20,000 administrative subpoena-type cases (i.e., NSLs) per year – even with a corresponding injection of resources and personnel – would fundamentally transform the nature of the FISC to the detriment of its current responsibilities.

- It is important that the process for selection of FISC and Court of Review judges remain both expeditious and fully confidential; the Chief Justice is uniquely positioned to select qualified judges for those Courts.

- In many cases, public disclosure of Court decisions is not likely to enhance the public's understanding of FISA implementation if the discussion of classified information within those opinions is withheld. Releasing freestanding summaries of Court opinions is likely to promote confusion and misunderstanding.

- Care should be taken not to place the Courts in an "oversight" role that exceeds their constitutional responsibility to decide cases and controversies.

Thank you for your previously expressed interest in the perspectives of the Judiciary on these matters. Although these comments are not intended as expressions of support or opposition to particular introduced bills, I hope they are helpful to Congress in its deliberations on potential legislation. We have also provided these comments to the Administration. If we can be of further assistance to you, please do not hesitate to contact me at 202-502-3000 or our Office of Legislative Affairs at 202-502-1700.

Sincerely,

John D. Bates
Director

Enclosure

Identical letter sent to: Honorable Patrick J. Leahy
           Honorable Dianne Feinstein
           Honorable Saxby Chambliss
           Honorable Bob Goodlatte
           Honorable John Conyers, Jr.
           Honorable Mike Rogers
           Honorable C.A. Dutch Ruppersberger

January 9, 2014

The Honorable Barack Obama
The White House
1600 Pennsylvania Avenue NW
Washington, DC 20500

Dear President Obama,

Amnesty International is deeply concerned that the US government's mass surveillance program violates the human right to privacy and threatens the rights to free expression and association as enshrined in international law.

As you consider changes to US surveillance policy, we urge you to take the following steps:

- Explain the purpose and disclose the scope of the US government's mass surveillance program.

- Ensure that US surveillance practices both inside and outside the United States are brought in line with international human rights standards, including the International Covenant on Civil and Political Rights.

- Publicly commit the US government to following the principles of legality, necessity, proportionality, due process, and transparency in any surveillance of communications. The International Principles on the Application of Human Rights to Communications Surveillance, available at https://en.necessaryandproportionate.org/text, provide guidance on implementation.

- Ensure that reform of US surveillance includes respect for the rights of people outside of US territory, as well as within.

- Establish a truly independent adversarial voice to champion privacy rights before the Foreign Intelligence Surveillance Court, and strengthen Congressional oversight of both the court and the NSA programs over which it has jurisdiction.

- Actively support, not undermine, efforts—including those of civil society—to create and maintain data encryption standards and effectively use encryption as a means to increase user security and trust.

- Recognize the right, indeed the duty, of federal employees to blow the whistle when they encounter evidence of human rights violations, and strengthen protections for whistleblowers.

In your May, 2013 speech on national security, you stated that "the decisions that we are making now will define the type of nation—and world—that we leave to our children." Respect for the human rights of all people is the cornerstone of a safe and free future. Accordingly, we urge you to make meaningful, human rights-centered reforms to US surveillance practices.

Sincerely,

Steven W. Hawkins
Executive Director
Amnesty International USA

Cc:

Lisa Monaco, Assistant to the President for Homeland Security and Counterterrorism
Stephen Pomper, Senior Director for Multilateral Affairs & Human Rights
John Kerry, Secretary of State
Samantha Power, US Ambassador to the United Nations
James R. Clapper, Director of National Intelligence
General Keith B. Alexander, Director of the National Security Agency
John Brennan, Director, Central Intelligence Agency
James B. Comey, Director of the Federal Bureau of Investigation

Connecting the Dots:
Analysis of the Effectiveness of Bulk Phone Records Collection

Marshall Erwin
Research Fellow • Hoover Institution

January 13, 2014

Under Section 215 of the USA PATRIOT Act, the National Security Agency (NSA) has pooled the phone records of millions of U.S. citizens into a massive data set. An accurate assessment of the program's effectiveness is necessary to make an informed judgment about the privacy tradeoffs entailed by this collection. The program's effectiveness as a counterterrorism tool is also important to its legal underpinnings. And to many Americans, what is more important than even legality or intrusiveness of this program is its value, or lack thereof, to our nation's security.

The topic of Section 215 effectiveness has been addressed often by outside legal experts and pundits, the vast majority of whom lack any counterterrorism or intelligence expertise. Intelligence officials have also commented on the topic, but the sensitivity of their positions prevents an in-depth discussion. This paper provides a discussion of the effectiveness of bulk records collection using a degree of rigor that has been lacking from both critics and proponents of this intelligence program.

Intelligence community officials have given two primary examples of the value or prospective value of Section 215 bulk phone records collection: the disrupted 2009 al-Qaeda plot targeting the New York City subway and the case of Khalid al-Mihdhar, the 9/11 hijacker who was under surveillance by NSA and who, the government alleges, could have been found if NSA had Section 215 authorities before the 9/11 attacks. Upon review of the facts of these two cases, neither is compelling. Bulk phone records collection would not have helped disrupt the 9/11 plot and did not make a significant contribution to success against the 2009 plot.

The analysis presented here is limited to the bulk phone records collection. Based upon records available to the public, there is little question that the collection of Internet-based communications using Section 702 authorities is effective and has immense benefits to national security. Many will raise other, broader objections to Section 702. It is important to raise those objections despite its effectiveness, rather than in ignorance of its effectiveness, and to be very careful when considering changes to that section of FISA.

But as for Section 215, an analysis of the facts demonstrates that the bulk phone records collection program is of marginal value.

The Case of Najibullah Zazi

To justify the bulk collection of American's phone records, intelligence officials repeatedly cite the disruption of a 2009 al-Qaeda plot, led by Najibullah Zazi, to bomb the New York City subway. Described as the single most important al-Qaeda plot over the last decade involving American citizens, this intelligence and law enforcement success undoubtedly saved many American lives. Zazi, who was born in Afghanistan and grew up in New York, traveled to Pakistan in the summer of 2008 and learned bomb-making techniques there. He moved to Denver upon his return to the United States in January 2009 and began to make preparations for an attack to take place sometime around September 11, 2009.

NSA did play a key role in disrupting this plot. Under Section 702 authorities, NSA intercepted emails between Zazi and an associate in Pakistan on September 6 and 7, 2009 that contained coded messages concerning the pending attack.[1] These emails were provided by NSA to the FBI and proved to be the critical lead that allowed the FBI to identify Zazi.

Proponents of bulk collection argue that Zazi's phone records, although less important than his emails, also contributed to this success. According to a recently released 2009 statement from the Director of the National Counterterrorism Center (NCTC) and the NSA Associate Deputy Director for Counterterrorism to the House Permanent Select Committee on Intelligence (HPSCI):

> "The FBI passed Zazi's mobile telephone number to NSA on the evening of 9 – 10 September [2009]... Shortly after receipt of Zazi's telephone number from FBI—and at approximately the same time that Zazi had obtained a one-way car rental from Colorado to New York City and had begun driving to New York—NSA issued a Business Records FISA metadata report on domestic and foreign contacts of that telephone. Among those contacts identified was a phone later confirmed as belonging to a key Zazi associate Adis Medunjanin. This was the FBI's first intelligence information about Medunjanin's telephone number and the contact corroborated other early information about Medunjanin's relationship with Zazi."[2]

---

[1] One email from the morning of September 7th stated that, "the marriage is ready flour and oil." 'Marriage' is often used as code for a pending attack and flour and oil are references to the chemicals used to make explosives. Transcript of Record, U.S. v. Zazi, No. 1:10-CR-60 (E.D.N.Y. July 18, 2011), available at http://www.scribd.com/doc/146422383/Zaz-i-Hearing.

[2] Michael Leiter and an unnamed NSA Associate Deputy Director, Joint Statement for the Record, the House Permanent Select Committee on Intelligence, Closed Hearing on Patriot Act Reauthorization, October 21, 2009, available at available at http://www.dni.gov/files/documents/501/NSA%20joint%20report%20(Oct%202009)_Sealed%20FINAL.pdf.

The argument here is twofold: 1) the phone records at NSA were important to linking Zazi to Medunjanin; and 2) the corroboration using the phone records was important to disrupting the plot because it "significantly accelerated and focused the investigation."[3] Both of these are highly questionable.

The FBI opened its investigation into Zazi on September 7, 2009, and began surveillance of Zazi's residence in Denver that evening.[4] Zazi departed for New York early on the morning of September 9, 2009. Authorities determined at around 7am that morning that he was driving to New York and began tailing Zazi as he traveled across the country.[5] FBI agents in New York were alerted to Zazi's travel at some point on September 9. If the government's timeline concerning the phone records query at NSA is accurate, this would indicate that the FBI had been surveilling Zazi for approximately two days, was aware of the seriousness of the threat he posed, and was following him on his drive to New York, all before the phone records were queried.

The key term used in the statement from the NCTC Director and NSA Associate Deputy Director is "corroborated other early information about Medunjanin's relationship with Zazi." Although it is not clear exactly what information had previously linked Medunjanin to Zazi, various public accounts suggest that the law enforcement and intelligence communities probably had two sources connecting the two men—travel records and an unnamed informant.

FBI Special Agent Eric Jurgenson, during testimony in the trial of Zazi's father, stated that one of the first steps taken in the investigation of Najibullah Zazi was to look at travel records.[6] As noted above, that investigation was opened on September 7, 2009. Those records show that Zazi and Medunjanin were on the same flight, Qatar Airways Flight 84, departing the Newark Liberty International Airport on August 28, 2008.[7] This was the first leg of their trip to training grounds in Pakistan. The two returned separately. That account is consistent with the one reported by Matt Apuzzo and Adam Goldman in their book *Enemies Within*, which states that by September 9, 2009, "Using flight manifests and seating charts, FBI analysts in Washington had concluded that Zazi probably had not traveled alone. They were confident that two others joined him: Zarein

[3] Ibid.
[4] Transcript of Record, U.S. v. Zazi, No. 1:10-CR-60 (E.D.N.Y. July 18, 2011).
[5] Special Agent Eric Jurgenson testified that, "In early morning hours of September 9th, 2009, Najibullah got in a rental car," Transcript of Record, U.S. v. Zazi, No. 1:10-CR-60 (E.D.N.Y. July 18, 2011). Zazi was stopped by the Colorado State Patrol at around 7am that morning an hour east of Denver, at which point authorities determined Zazi's destination, according to Matt Apuzzo and Adam Goldman, *Enemies Within*, Simon & Schuster, Inc. 2013, p. 11.
[6] Transcript of Record, U.S. v. Zazi, No. 1:10-CR-60 (E.D.N.Y. July 18, 2011).
[7] Ibid.

Ahmedzay, a New York taxi driver, and Adis Medunjanin, a security guard in Manhattan."[8]

The FBI or another intelligence agency also appears to have had a source or sources that had previously linked Zazi to Medunjanin. Press accounts of a 2011 evidentiary hearing against Medunjanin indicate that an intelligence agency source was with Zazi and Medunjanin in Pakistan and helped them gain access to a training camp there.[9] The testimony of FBI Deputy Director Sean Joyce in a July 2013 hearing before the Senate Judiciary Committee also referenced a source who linked Zazi to Medunjanin.[10] There is no further public information to indicate whether these are different references to the same source or to indicate how much the FBI knew about Medunjanin before September 2009. We do know that the FBI was already investigating one of Medunjanin's associates as of September 9, 2009.[11]

At the point when NSA utilized its bulk phone records collection program, the FBI was well on its way to disrupting Zazi's plot, appears to have had sufficient information to do so, and had already linked Zazi to Medunjanin. This does not mean that the phone records played no role in this success. Any additional piece of information that provided insight into the relationship between the two men could have had some value. But the important operative question is whether the plot would have been disrupted without the phone records database. A reasonable analysis of the facts suggests that the answer is yes.

9/11 and the Case of Khalid al-Mihdhar

The second case for Section 215 bulk phone records collections concerns Khalid al-Mihdhar, the 9/11 hijacker who some argue would have been captured if the bulk phone records collection program had been in place before the attack. For example, according to the same 2009 statement to HPSCI:

---

[8] *Enemies Within*, p. 9.

[9] Mosi Secret, "Homegrown Bomb Plot is Rarity for Open Court," *The New York Times*, April 15, 2012, available at http://www.nytimes.com/2012/04/16/nyregion/revelations-expected-in-trial-of-adis-medunjanin-a-terror-suspect.html.

[10] U.S. Congress, Senate Judiciary Committee, Strengthening Privacy Rights and National Security: Oversight of FISA Surveillance, July 31, 2013. Senator Leahy, in the context of a discussion about the role of Section 215 collection in the disruption of the Zazi plot, asked "Wasn't there some undercover work that took place?" FBI Deputy Director Sean Joyce responded, "Yes, there was some undercover work."

[11] Michael Leiter and an unnamed NSA Associate Deputy Director, Joint Statement for the Record, the House Permanent Select Committee on Intelligence, Closed Hearing on Patriot Act Reauthorization, October 21, 2009.

(TS//SI//NF) Members will recall that, prior to the attacks of 9/11, the NSA intercepted and transcribed seven calls from hijacker Khalid al-Mihdhar to a facility associated with an al Qa'ida safehouse in Yemen. However, NSA's access point overseas did not provide the technical data indicating where al-Mihdhar was calling from. Lacking the originating phone number, and hearing nothing in the content of those calls to suggest he was in the United States, NSA analysts concluded that al-Mihdhar was overseas. In fact, al-Mihdhar was calling from San Diego, California. According to the 9/11 Commission Report (pages 269-272):

> "Investigations or interrogation of them [Khalid al-Mihdhar, etc], and investigation of their travel and financial activities could have yielded evidence of connections to other participants in the 9/11 plot. The simple fact of their detention could have derailed the plan. In any case, the opportunity did not arise." [1]

[12]

Proponents of bulk phone collection argue that if NSA had had such a tool before 9/11, it would have been able to determine whether the phone number in Yemen had been in contact with a domestic number. Analysts would have then determined that al-Mihdhar was in the United States and could have alerted the FBI.

Bulk phone records collection *could* have allowed the intelligence community to stop the 9/11 attacks, but an experienced intelligence analyst will tell you that there is a gulf between *could* and *would*. A comprehensive assessment of the publicly available information about al-Mihdhar leads to the conclusion that the phone records would not have made a difference. The full history of lost opportunities regarding al-Mihdhar is not necessary here, as the 9/11 Commission and other investigations have provided extensive treatments of the subject. These investigations demonstrate that the intelligence and law enforcement communities had ample opportunity to identify al-Mihdhar and to disrupt the 9/11 plot, yet failed to do so.

The CIA as of early 2000 was aware of al-Mihdhar's affiliation with al-Qaeda, aware that he was in possession of a U.S. visa, and aware that one of his close associates (fellow hijacker Nawaf al-Hazmi) had traveled to the United States. The CIA did not provide this information to the FBI until soon before the 9/11 attacks.[13] When he arrived in San Diego, al-Mihdhar also had frequent contact with an FBI asset and rented a room in the home of that asset.[14]

Notably, al-Mihdhar appears to have made some of his seven calls to Yemen *from the FBI asset's home*. This is clear from an analysis of his travels and a timeline of those

[12] Michael Leiter and an unnamed NSA Associate Deputy Director, Joint Statement for the Record, the House Permanent Select Committee on Intelligence, Close Hearing on Patriot Act Reauthorization, October 21, 2009.

[13] U.S. National Commission on Terrorist Attacks Upon the United States, *The 9/11 Commission Report*, July 2004. p. 182.

[14] Ibid, p. 220. See also chapter five of U.S. Department of Justice, Office of Inspector General, *A Review of the FBI's Handling of Intelligence Information Related to the September 11 Attacks*, June, 2006, p. 259.

calls but is never stated explicitly by the 9/11 Commission or by those advocating for bulk phone records collection. Al-Mihdhar moved into the home of the asset on May 10, 2000, and departed on June 9, 2000.[15] The 9/11 Commission refers to multiple calls made to the Yemen safehouse from al-Mihdhar's residence soon before his departure from the United States that June.[16] Other calls appear to have taken place before May 10.[17]

To justify Section 215 bulk collection, intelligence community documents delivered to Congress and to the Foreign Intelligence Surveillance Court (FISC) often cite al-Mihdhar's communications with the al-Qaeda safehouse in Yemen.[18] As demonstrated above, these documents then immediately quote the 9/11 Commission report. This would seem to suggest that the Commission found that shortcomings of NSA phone records collection were critical. In fact, the quote reproduce above has been taken out of context. The seven pages about al-Mihdhar that precede the quote are dedicated to information sharing problems between the CIA and the FBI and do not identify NSA's records collection as a core problem.

Roughly twenty-nine pages of the *9/11 Commission Report* are dedicated to al-Mihdhar, his travels, and opportunities for his capture.[19] One sentence on page 222 in the body of the report appears to reference the communications at issue in the debate over Section 215 authorities.[20] The report does list ten operational opportunities related to al-Mihdhar and his associate, Nawaf al-Hazmi, that could have allowed intelligence and law enforcement officials to disrupt the attack.[21] Problems associated with NSA's collection of al-Mihdhar's communications did not make the list.

The Department of Justice Inspector General report on the FBI's handling of intelligence related to the 9/11 attacks spends 139 pages specifically discussing al-Mihdhar and al-Hazmi and related information sharing problems between the FBI and other members of

---

[15] *The 9/11 Commission Report*, p. 220. The report states that al-Hazmi and al-Mihdhar found a room in the home of an individual they had met at a mosque in San Diego, moving in on May 9th. Page 314 of the DOJ Inspector General report on the FBI's handling of intelligence related to 9/11 states that this was the home of the FBI asset.

[16] According to page 222 of the *9/11 Commission Report*, "Al-Mihdhar's mind seems to have been with his family back in Yemen, as evidenced by calls he made from the apartment telephone. When news of the birth of his first child arrived, he could stand life in California no longer. In late May and early June of 2000, he closed his bank account, transferred the car registration to Al-Hazmi, and arranged his return to Yemen." This indicates he was calling home from the FBI asset's home in May 2000.

[17] The report from the Department of Justice's Office of Inspector General on the FBI's handling of intelligence related to the 9/11 attacks states that one of the calls to Yemen took place on March 20th. *A Review of the FBI's Handling of Intelligence Information Related to the September 11 Attacks*, June, 2006, p. 251.

[18] See, for example, U.S. Department of Justice, Office of Legislative Affairs, *Report on the National Security Agency's Bulk Collection Program for USA PATRIOT Act Reauthorization*, February 2, 2011, available at http://www.dni.gov/files/documents/2009_CoverLetter_Report_Collection.pdf.

[19] This includes pages 181, 155 – 160, 215 – 223, 237, 240, 266 – 272, and 353 – 357.

[20] *The 9/11 Commission Report*, p. 222.

[21] Ibid., pp. 355 – 356.

the intelligence community.[22] The communications at issue in the Section 215 debate are briefly referenced in two sentences on page 259 of the report.[23] The report specifically lists five missed opportunities for the FBI to learn about al-Mihdhar and al-Hazmi, including cases in which intelligence reporting could have been shared with the FBI. Problems associated with NSA's collection of al-Mihdhar's communications did not make the list.[24]

More than twenty-six pages of the report from the congressional Joint Inquiry into the 9/11 attacks are dedicated to al-Mihdhar and his associates.[25] This includes several references—roughly a page of material in total[26]—to NSA surveillance of al-Mihdhar's communications from San Diego and a more explicit discussion of NSA's inability to locate the source of Al-Mihdhar's calls:

> While the Intelligence Community had information regarding these communications [between al-Mihdhar and the safehouse in Yemen], it did not determine the location from which they had been made...After September 11, the FBI determined from domestic [phone] records that it was in fact the hijacker Khalid al-Mihdhar who had made these communications and that he had done so from within the United States. The Intelligence Community did not identify what was critically important information in terms of the domestic threat to the United States: the fact that the communications were between individuals within the United States and suspected terrorist facilities overseas. That kind of information could have provided crucial investigative leads to law enforcement agencies engaged in domestic counterterrorism efforts.[27]

As compared to the reports discussed above, the Joint Inquiry more clearly identifies al-Mihdhar's spring 2000 communications as a missed opportunity to disrupt the plot. Again, this should be understood in the context of other problems identified in the report. Eleven pages of the Joint Inquiry's discussion of al-Mihdhar focus on his contact with the FBI asset. Several pages discuss the CIA's failure to watchlist al-Mihdhar and to share sufficiently with the FBI. NSA is also criticized in the report for failing to disseminate information in its possession about al-Mihdhar to other members of the community, a problem unrelated to technical limitations of its collection.

In sum, post-9/11 investigations show that the intelligence community had sufficient information about al-Mihdhar to disrupt the attack but not sufficient initiative, largely as

---

[22] See chapter five of U.S. Department of Justice, Office of Inspector General, *A Review of the FBI's Handling of Intelligence Information Related to the September 11 Attacks,* June, 2006.
[23] Ibid, p. 259.
[24] Ibid. p. 313.
[25] A more exact page count is not possible because portions of the Joint Inquiry's report are redacted.
[26] See pages 16 - 17, 157, and 248 in the Joint Inquiry's report. U.S. Congress, the U.S. Senate Select Committee on Intelligence and U.S. House Permanent Select Committee on Intelligence, *Joint Inquiry into Intelligence Community Activities Before and After the Terrorist Attacks of September 11, 2001.* December 2002. 107th Congress, 2nd session (H.Rept. 107-792). [Also, S.Rept. 107-351]
[27] Ibid., p. 16.

a result of cultural barriers and other institutional impediments within different intelligence agencies. The congressional Joint Inquiry does suggest that bulk phone collection *could have* helped disrupt the attack, but the majority of its discussion of al-Mihdhar is dedicated to other missed opportunities. After the attack, the FBI was able to quickly identify the domestic source of calls to the al-Qaeda safehouse in Yemen, further demonstrating that the failure to locate al-Mihdhar was not truly a problem resulting from NSA collection or limits on FISA authorities. To suggest that one additional piece of information before the attack *would have* made a difference is incorrect.

Open Questions Concerning al-Mihdhar

Two issues may warrant further review and could provide additional insight into the prospective role of bulk phone records in the al-Mihdhar case.

The congressional Joint Inquiry criticized NSA for failing to disseminate al-Mihdhar's communications with his wife in Yemen. It does not indicate, at least in its unredacted text, why these communications could have been useful if they had been disseminated outside of NSA. One possible explanation of their prospective value may be that they provide contextual clues to indicate al-Mihdhar's presence in the United States. Given his dissatisfaction with the United States and his pending return to Yemen, it seems possible that these communications may reference his location. The statement above from the NCTC Director and NSA Associate Deputy Director indicates that this is not the case. An unredacted version of the Joint Inquiry report or a review of intercepts of al-Mihdhar may provide insights into this issue.

Lawrence Wright, in *The Looming Tower*, writes that, "The NSA, not wanting to bother with applying to the FISA court for permission to distribute essential intelligence, simply restricted its distribution [of communications between al-Mihdhar and the safehouse in Yemen]."[28] This would suggest NSA was aware of al-Mihdhar's location. The 9/11 Commission similarly concludes that, "[W]hile NSA had the technical capability to report on communication with suspected terrorist facilities in the Middle East, the NSA did not seek FISA Court warrants to collect communications between individuals in the United States and foreign countries, because it believed that this was an FBI role."[29] This may be a reference to al-Mihdhar's communications. The Commission does not further elaborate on the topic. These accounts are inconsistent with the Joint Inquiry and would indicate that NSA had the means, but not the inclination, to collect al-Mihdhar's records. That is, the agency knew (or could have known) al-Mihdhar's location, but chose not to use that capability to gather and disseminate intelligence about his communications.

---

[28] Lawrence Write, *The Looming Tower: Al-Qaeda and the Road to 9/11*, Random House, 2006, p. 343.
[29] *The 9/11 Commission Report*, pp. 87 – 88.

Cases of Terrorist Facilitation

Intelligence officials have described twelve "terrorism events"—cases of either terrorist plots targeting the U.S. homeland or terrorist facilitation somehow linked to the homeland—in which the bulk phone records at NSA contributed to the disruption of terrorist activity. NSA Director General Alexander, in a hearing before the Senate Judiciary Committee on December 11, 2013, further elaborated on this claim. He stated that of these twelve, there is one case in which Section 215 played a unique role, seven in which it contributed, and four in which the phone records did not have value.[30] Intelligence officials have separately identified the case of Basaaly Moalin, a San Diego-based man who in 2007 and early 2008 coordinated fundraising efforts for al Shabaab, the Somali extremist group that merged with al-Qaeda in 2012. Presumably, the Zazi case is one of the seven in which the phone records are alleged to have contributed. That leaves six additional cases in which the phone records played a role but about which we know very little.

There is no basis upon which to judge the government's assertions regarding these six unidentified cases and, in such circumstances where details are sensitive and classified, it is reasonable to assume that those assertions are accurate. It is also reasonable to conclude, however, that these are probably not plots targeting the U.S. homeland and that the majority are instances of terrorist facilitation, like the Moalin case, rather than active terrorist plotting against the homeland.[31] If these were disrupted terror plots targeting the U.S. homeland, individuals would likely have been prosecuted and details would have almost certainly come to light even before the unauthorized disclosure of phone records collection this summer. This is exactly what happened with the Zazi case. Further, given the intense pressure NSA is under, these details would have been disclosed in recent months.

The question this raises is whether the one case of terrorist facilitation in which Section 215 records played a unique role and the six cases in which they played some role justify the collection and retention of most Americans' phone records. This becomes a

---

[30] U.S. Congress, Senate Judiciary Committee, Oversight of Surveillance Agencies, 113th Congress, 1st sess., December 11, 2013.

[31] NSA Deputy Director John Inglis stated in a July 31, 2013, hearing before the Senate Judiciary Committee that Section 215 made a contribution to a plot that was disrupted overseas. Recent FBI submissions in two lawsuits challenging the constitutionality of bulk phone records collection have identified two additional cases in which the bulk phone records were used; a 2009 plot to bomb the New York Stock Exchange and a 2009 plot against a Danish newspaper. It is not clear whether these two were included in the set of twelve identified earlier by intelligence officials. The FBI's submissions are carefully word and suggest the phone records played a marginal role in both cases. See page 10 of Declaration of Acting Assistant Director Robert J. Holley, Federal Bureau of Investigation, October 1, 2013, available at https://www.aclu.org/files/assets/2013.10.01_govt_oppn_to_pi_motion_-_holley_declaration.pdf. Intelligence officials have not otherwise distinguished between terror plots and terrorism facilitation when discussing the remaining undisclosed terrorist events in which the bulk phone records were used.

subjective policy judgment that depends on one's sensitivity to privacy and security concerns.

The Challenge of Layered Defense Against Terrorism

There does not appear to be a case in which Section 215 bulk phone records played an important role in stopping a terrorist attack.[32] In light of this fact, intelligence community officials have also argued that the absence of such an example does not indicate that the program lacks value. NSA General Counsel Rajesh De, in a November 2013 hearing before the Privacy and Civil Liberties Oversight Board, argued that "From the intelligence community's perspective, intelligence is a function that is brought together by a lot of different tools that work in complement to one another and I'd also…suggest that [for] any particular plot, it is rare that you are going to find a situation were some particular event was only unearthed or only stopped as a result of one particular intelligence tool."[33]

This is a fair characterization of the intelligence process. The problem with the argument is that it can be used to justify even useless intelligence and counterterrorism programs. It is a mistake to suggest that because good intelligence work is the result of the synthesis of many difference tools, we cannot ask hard questions about the effectiveness of any particular tool. Further, it is somewhat inconsistent with the facts of the Najibullah Zazi case. Multiple accounts of the disruption of that plot indicate emails sent from Zazi to an individual in Pakistan and collected by NSA provided the critical lead that tipped the U.S. government off about the plot. The email address of Zazi's contact was originally collected and provided to NSA by our partners in the United Kingdom, and the emails sent from Zazi and shared by NSA prompted swift action from the FBI.[34] Thus, the success there was the result of the synthesis of different tools. But that does not diminish the singular role that emails collected using Section 702 authorities played in that case. We simply do not have a similar example where bulk phone records were nearly as critical.

In response to the terrorist attacks on 9/11, the Untied States put in place a layered system of defense, involving multiple overlapping tools and agencies working in concert. This system has accomplished its ultimate goal of saving American lives. Policymakers should

---

[32] This is a conclusion shared by the President's Review Group on Intelligence and Communications Technologies, which found that "Section 215 telephony meta-data was not essential to preventing attacks and could readily have been obtained in a timely manner using conventional section 215 order."

[33] Rajesh De, comments before the Privacy and Civil Liberties Oversight Board, November 4, 2013, available at http://www.pclob.gov/SiteAssets/PCLOB%20Hearing%20-%20Full%20Day%20transcript%20Nov%204%202013.pdf. See also Matthew Waxmen's "How to Measure the Value of NSA Programs," Lawfare, August 12, 2013, available at http://www.lawfareblog.com/2013/08/how-to-measure-the-value-of-nsa-programs/.

[34] *Enemies Within*, p. 54. The email address of Zazi's contact in Pakistan was collected by the British Secret Service in spring 2009.

therefore proceed with care as they consider curtailing certain authorities, for fear of weakening the integrity of the entire system. But they can nonetheless expect better of our intelligence and counterterrorism communities. Indeed, few with "on-the-ground" experience in the counterterrorism efforts of the last decade will argue that the system currently in place is smart or efficient. The system works but it does not work well. It has layers of redundancy that add value and layers that add little, tools that help find al-Qaeda leaders and tools that largely serve to take up computer memory at billion-dollar data centers.

This theme is echoed in the recent report from the President's Review Group on Intelligence and Communications Technologies, which found that, "In many areas of public policy, officials are increasingly insistent on the need for careful analysis of the consequences of their decisions, and on the importance of relying not on intuitions and anecdotes, but on evidence and data."[35] The Review Group recommendation that significant changes be made to the bulk phone records collection program suggests that a careful analysis of the evidence supporting the program had not been performed previously and that such an analysis does not support the program as it is currently implemented.

In an age of austerity and with 9/11 receding into history, a failure to justify our current counterterrorism tools and structure and to make them smarter will itself threaten the integrity of our counterterrorism efforts, as Americans look with growing skepticism at the entire intelligence apparatus. This is exactly what we see occurring with NSA now as important programs for national security have come under as much criticism as those of marginal value. If we want to ensure the long-term viability of counterterrorism efforts and our continued success against al-Qaeda, we must increasingly prune away those programs and activities that have not helped keep us safe.

Marshall Erwin is a Research Fellow at the Hoover Institution. He previously served as the intelligence specialist at the Congressional Research Service, as a professional staff member on the Senate Homeland Security and Government Affairs Committee, and as a counterterrorism analyst in the intelligence community.

---

[35] "Liberty and Security in a Changing World," Report and Recommendations of the President's Review Group in Intelligence and Communications Technologies," December 12, 2013, p. 16.

The Wall Street Journal

Mukasey: The Air of Unreality in NSA Reform

The president's panel found no official malfeasance but recommends overhauling surveillance programs anyway.

By Michael B. Mukasey

Dec. 23, 2013 7:19 p.m. ET

Grope through the Styrofoam pellets of rhetoric that surround the 46 recommendations in the report issued last week by the president's Review Group on Intelligence and Communications Technologies, and you will discover that the authors "have not uncovered any official efforts to suppress dissent or any intent to intrude into people's private lives without legal justification." The panel's investigation of the National Security Agency found—as the Foreign Intelligence Surveillance Court found before them—that the occasional unintentional violations of guidelines were stopped once they were detected.

Yet in a Dec. 20 White House news conference, President Obama vowed that next month he will make a "pretty definitive statement" about surveillance reform based on the panel's recommendations. The five-member group, including University of Chicago law professor Geoffrey Stone and Harvard Law School professor Cass Sunstein, was appointed by the president in August amid the continuing fallout from the theft of national-security secrets by former government contractor Edward Snowden.

If the presidential Review Group found no official malfeasance, what has generated the 46 recommendations for reform? The answer seems to lie more in the mind-set of those commissioned to examine the intelligence programs than in the programs themselves.

The panel scrutinized principally an NSA program that gathers telephone metadata (which show the calling and called numbers, the date and the length of the call), and one that monitors the communications non-U.S. persons abroad.

Outside the National Security Agency headquarters in Fort Meade, Md. Patrick Semansky/Associated Press

Telephone metadata collection allows investigators to run the known number of a foreign terrorist, say, or of a safe house, against a database of U.S. calls to determine whether that number has called or been called by any domestic number. If so, investigators could then focus on that telephone and, if further evidence were sufficient, obtain a warrant to tap the content of conversations.

The constitutionality of the procedure has been upheld repeatedly. And as the panel noted, the "NSA believes that on at least a few occasions, information derived from the . . . metadata program has contributed to its efforts to prevent possible terrorist attacks either in the United States or somewhere else in the world."

The Review Group's report couldn't point to an actual invasion of privacy from NSA's collection of telephone metadata. Yet, astoundingly, the panel recommends that the program be terminated with a transition "as soon as reasonably possible to a system in which such meta-data is held instead either by private providers or by a private third party."

In other words, if investigators want to check a telephone number they should be required to scurry around to each individual provider— AT&T, T +0.31% Verizon, etc.—to run the check, possibly against data bases that are inconsistently arranged, with consequent loss of time and efficiency. What if this arrangement "seriously undermines the effectiveness of the program," as well as national security? The panel suggests that "the government *might* authorize a specially designated private organization to collect and store the bulk telephony metadata" (emphasis added).

The panel, in short, is recommending an experiment: If there is serious damage to the program—measured, say, by a successful terrorist attack—well, then we can have the data placed in the hands of a private party, and we know nothing can go wrong with that.

The president's Review Group offers two reasons why the NSA must not gather this telephone metadata. One is that the government might use the business-records rationale for gathering metadata to cull other sensitive personal information in medical records and the like. Of course, no evidence suggests that any such thing has been tried or even contemplated by anyone in authority.

The second reason offered for terminating the NSA program is that telephone metadata can be mined to construct a profile of a particular person—who that person has called and who has called that person—and the possibility of that occurring would unsettle many people if they thought it was being done to them. No evidence suggests that any such thing has been proposed or done, and indeed the 22 people at NSA who have access to the data are forbidden to use metadata in any fashion other than to run it against suspect telephone numbers.

Nonetheless, the panel finds that mere public awareness of potential abuse "can significantly undermine public trust, which is exceedingly important to the well-being of a free and open society." To be sure, the panel recommends that the government "commission a study of the legal and policy options for assessing the distinction between metadata and other types of information." But in the meantime, the NSA would cease to collect telephone metadata.

What about gathering electronic intelligence abroad? The panel reasons that although the law authorizing that activity "has clearly served an important function in helping the United States to uncover and prevent terrorist attacks both in the United States and around the world (and thus helps protect our allies), the question remains whether it achieves that goal in a way that unnecessarily sacrifices individual privacy and damages foreign relations."

Here too the panel finds the NSA wanting—for failure to uphold Article 12 of the Universal Declaration of Human Rights and Article 17 of the International Covenant on Civil and Political Rights, which "proclaim that 'No one shall be subjected to arbitrary or unlawful interference with his privacy.' Although that declaration provides little guidance about what is meant by 'arbitrary or unlawful interference,' the aspiration is clear. The United States should be a leader in championing . . . the right of privacy, which is central to human dignity." Based on that "clear" aspiration, the Review Group recommends that protections of the Privacy Act of 1974 be extended even by intelligence-gathering agencies to non-U.S. persons so as to permit them, for example, to discover the personally identifiable information in their intelligence file, "unless the agencies provide specific and persuasive reasons not to do so."

Oh, sure—it's hard to imagine what "specific and persuasive" reason there might be not to allow a foreign terrorist to check on whether the U.S. government has a file on him and what may be in it.

Another recommendation: The U.S. should declare that surveillance abroad "must not target any non-United States person located outside of the United States based solely on that person's political views or religious convictions." So, for example, if a previously unknown group declares it a religious obligation to kill Americans, we must promise not to target that group or its leaders for surveillance to determine whether they have the operational capability to put their "political views or religious convictions" into practice. Makes sense.

And what about the National Security Agency itself? The president wisely has already rejected the panel's idea that the director of NSA no longer head the U.S. Cyber Command. But the panel also advocates separating the NSA from Cyber Command, and detaching the NSA's information-assurance (code-making) function from its foreign-intelligence (code breaking) function. Why? Because after the 9/11 terror attacks, many in government advocated new national-security measures, and "if a similar or worse incident . . . were to occur in the future, many Americans, in the fear and heat of the moment, might support new restrictions on civil liberties and privacy. The powerful existing and potential capabilities of our intelligence and law enforcement agencies might be unleashed without adequate controls." Better to break up a successful team than risk that.

No doubt such airy reasoning, not to mention arrogant mistrust of this country's citizens and its institutions, is the small change of daily discourse in faculty lounges. But to find this infiltrating the Situation Room of the White House—President Obama met with the Review Group there before leaving on his Hawaiian vacation—is truly alarming.

Mr. Mukasey served as U.S. attorney general (2007-09) and as a U.S. district judge for the Southern District of New York (1988-2006).

76

Submissions for the record not printed due to voluminous nature, previously printed by an agency of the Federal Government, or other criteria determined by the Committee, list:

Report of the President's Review Group on Intelligence and Communication Technologies:

> http://www.whitehouse.gov/sites/default/files/docs/2013-12-12_rg_final_report.pdf

New America Foundation: ''Do NSA's Bulk Surveillance Programs Stop Terrorists?'' by Peter Bergen, David Sterman, Emily Schneider, and Bailey Cahall:

> http://www.newamerica.net/sites/newamerica.net/files/policydocs/Bergen_NAF_NSA%20Surveillance_1_0_0.pdf

Center for Security Policy, Occasional Paper Series: ''A Critique of the Recommendations by the President's Review Group on Intelligence and Communication Technologies'':

> http://www.centerforsecuritypolicy.org/wp-content/uploads/2014/01/NSA_report.pdf

''Comments on the Judiciary on Proposals Regarding the Foreign Intelligence Surveillance Act'' by John D. Bates, Director of the Administrative Office of the United States Courts:

> http://www.lawfareblog.com/wp-content/uploads/2014/01-10-2014-Enclosure-re-FISA.pdf

www.ingramcontent.com/pod-product-compliance
Lightning Source LLC
Chambersburg PA
CBHW081136290526
45795CB00006B/2260